Finding Quiet Strength © 2022 Judith Kleinman
Judith Kleinman is hereby identified as the author of this work in accordance with section 77 of the Copyright, Designs and Patent Act, 1988. She asserts and gives notice of her moral right under this Act.

Published by Quickthorn,
Hawthorn House, 1 Lansdown Lane, Stroud,
Gloucestershire, GL5 1BJ UK
Tel: (01453) 757040
info@quickthornbooks.com
www.quickthornbooks.com

All rights reserved. No part of this book may be reproduced, stored in a retrieval system or transmitted in any form by any means (electronic or mechanical, through reprography, digital transmission, recording or otherwise) without prior written permission of the publisher.

Editor: Katy Bevan
Design and Typesetting: Chris J Bailey
Printed by Short Run Press, Exeter

Printed in the UK on uncoated
FSC certified paper

British Library Cataloguing in Publication Data applied for
ISBN 978-1-912480-73-9

Finding Quiet Strength

emotional intelligence

embodied awareness

judith kleinman

Contents

Foreword   4

Who this book is for   9

Introduction and welcome   11

Calm
The embodied mind   19

Confidence
Structure and breath   41

Coordinated movement
The embodied sense of movement and ease   87

Curiosity
Integrating our senses   123

Creativity and purpose
Empowering our energy   147

Courage and conclusion
A quiet revolution   155

About the author   159

Further reading   160

Finding Quiet Strength

Foreword

Rather than asking one person to introduce the ideas in this book, I thought I would bring together some voices from students, colleagues and friends about this work and how it is relevant to all walks of life. I wanted to highlight how finding quiet strength – though it begins with the relationship with yourself – can help you to be calm and confident with others. Abi Wright, a friend and colleague, catches the urgency and huge potential of this work in education and in society:

When societal expectations encourage our girls to make themselves smaller to fit in and be accepted, we need to show them how to stand tall and own their space. We need to help them to feel at home in their bodies, to feel confident in who they are. We need to guide them towards finding quiet strength. Only when we allow this shift to happen can we move closer to a more gender equal society.

Abi Wright, *founder of She Stands and co-founder of Festival of The Girl*

Felicity Matthews, a viola player as well as my Alexander Technique teaching colleague, brilliantly shows how being peaceful in our bodies can help us connect with others:

I've noticed that when I ignore my nervous system being on high alert, I feel totally overwhelmed, anxious and more likely to have irritable or confrontational outbursts. When I'm feeling overwhelmed like this, connecting into the ground and actually seeing the room around me calms my nervous system and makes me more available to then connect in a calmer (and more reasonable!) way with others.

Felicity Matthews, *viola player ROH and Alexander Technique teacher*

I think this is such an important message and one that crosses disciplines. Lotte Bredt MBACP discusses how she applies these ideas in her counselling:

This work has taught me over the years that the very first, and by no means easy task is to notice what's going on inside the body/mind rather than rushing to change anything. This is a profound principle, which counteracts the rather ferocious demand to change our age-old bad habits.

As a psychotherapist I get excited every time patients discover for themselves that being able to pay attention to unhelpful patterns is already a sign of change. This work and psychoanalysis have in common that both make us aware of our embodied self in its spatial and temporal dimensions,

which connects us to our fellow humans and the world around us. In other words, moving and being moved physically and emotionally starts from a place of stillness.

So, this is also a grateful testimony to Judith Kleinman, my teacher of many years, who has taught me – in more than one way – to 'sit well' with myself and my patients.

Lotte Bredt, *MBACP counsellor and psychotherapist*

Something I find really valuable in this quote is that Lotte is using this work to compliment her own techniques and training. Finding quiet strength is not meant to be the right way to do something, it is intended to give us the means to choose how we do what we do with maximum freedom.

This can be particularly useful in performance activities where we are bringing our physical and mental preparation into a new and potentially pressurised situation. Andy Smith describes how valuable this can be to sports people:

Sport is full of opportunities to give ourselves more time and space, to think in activity and to think in stillness. We could, for example, utilise a moment of space before taking a penalty to consciously quieten our thoughts, check our breathing and stay in control of our nerves. We could also think on-the-go by encouraging muscular and mental release during a long bike ride or allow ourselves a split second of body awareness in the middle of a tennis rally. No matter what the situation is, the benefits are multiple: they all lead to easier movement, greater coordination and an inner calmness that can't fail to improve performance.

Andy Smith, *Alexander Technique teacher and RunSmart practitioner*

Violinist Madeleine Mitchell identifies that same quiet strength in the body as an essential part of performing music expressively:

In my work as a solo violinist, chamber musician and teacher internationally for over three decades, I've found good body use to be centrally important. Being aware of breathing, finding balance, ease and quiet inner strength, especially at very demanding times such as live broadcasts, is invaluable. This can enable the music to have free expression and let us be a channel for it in the moment of performance.

Madeleine Louise Mitchell, *violin soloist*

Foreword

A common thread throughout these quotes is the connection between an inner stillness or quiet strength and a sense of freedom and agency. We find that freedom within ourselves from a sense of inner quiet. I'm very grateful for Sarah Oliver's writing about this work, particularly in how she highlights such a fundamental topic, self-acceptance:

Finding quiet strength is a capability within us all, however, what is important is learning how to access it, and even more importantly practise it, so these skills are available to us all the time, especially when we need it the most.

In life we often think we have it all planned out; on some level we take comfort in thinking we know what's going to happen. At least, we think we know and then something else happens instead. Finding quiet strength is what we all need to be able to journey through our lives. We may not know what's going to happen in life but with this approach, we can know we'll find the strength to face whatever life throws at us.

I've come to learn the hard way that a prerequisite for finding quiet strength is to know you are enough as you are. It's from that place of deep acceptance that you will find the quiet strength within you. If this doesn't come naturally to you (and let's be honest, you are most definitely not alone with that), you can use the practices that Judith has described to find the place where you can feel safe enough, to build your resilience, to find your strength so that you can deal with anything that life throws at you.

Knowing I was already several years into learning and practising the skills to find the quiet strength that Judith embodies and has shared with us through this book was of immense comfort to me as I faced my toughest challenge to date. In 2020, I had brain surgery to remove a tumour and needed to recover physically, mentally and emotionally from the trauma. Developing these skills literally saved me – I don't know how I would have recovered without knowing these practices.

The wonderful advantage of the practices in Judith's book, which help you to find your quiet strength, is that they are immediately accessible and practical... you can practise them any place, anywhere and at any time. As soon as you can notice that you don't feel comfortable or are perhaps dealing with a difficult situation (or anticipating one) you can practise any of the strategies immediately and without it being obvious to anyone else! It's like packing a rucksack with your own personal life survival kit!

Sarah Oliver, *Alexander Technique teacher and Cornille Science of Motion practitioner*

One of my students had this reflection: Our work together has brought me awareness of the space within the body and the space outside the body, each side or part of the body being as important as any

Here Penny O'Connor makes the point that if we only identify ourselves with our thoughts and emotions, we might miss the chance to choose to connect.

So much of the time we are narrowed in our thinking, locked inside our own habitual perceptions, unable to change, though we do our best to concentrate hard, try to get things right, please others and strive busily and ineffectively. We have forgotten the golden rule to stop, to raise our head to the sky, to allow our eyes to see and breathe in the beauty of the world around us that sustains us, to sense the ground under our feet, our very existence stemming from and dependent on this living blue jewel, hurtling through the cold stars. Finding quiet strength, we can be reunited with the rapture of living, connecting in a profound way to the Earth and all that is in it.

Penny O'Connor, *author of* Alexander Technique for Actors

I'd like to thank my generous colleagues for taking the time to write these thoughts. It is good to be part of a community of people who think, experiment and practise ways to live life with peace and freedom in themselves and with others.

I would also like to say thank you to our son Harry for all his help with the script and to Peter and Abe for their support and good humour along the way. Also many thanks to my friend Katy B for encouraging me to write the book in the first place.

Who this book is for

Perhaps you bought this book because you would like to find a little more calm in your life. Perhaps you are looking for a sense of strength that isn't confrontational. Or maybe discomfort or pain is distracting you from being present. Sometimes we simply feel like we can't take the time out of our lives to have a moment to ourselves. This book is about finding embodied calm, flexibility and strength that means we have a sense of inner space and ease in our lives.

While I was a music student, I was seriously injured in a car accident. After that, I needed to learn the skills of recovery, how to find comfort in my body and, as I became stronger, how to unlearn the habits I had developed when I was vulnerable. During this process I began having Alexander

Technique lessons and practising yoga and tai chi, and these disciplines have become fundamental to the way in which I approach playing and performing music and life in general.

The most important skills I needed as a musician were how to deal with the pressure and the adrenaline of a performance, how to carry preparation into the situation, how to calm my nerves and how to engage with a large group of people even when feeling nervous. As I went through the ups and downs of life, the techniques I used in these situations were also a wonderful resource for much more than just performance; they have helped me balance the pressures of everyday life, find good boundaries and more resilience. I began to manage my energy well and become better able to relax and appreciate the joys of life.

The work can be applicable to every walk of life. My students have come from professions as diverse as music, architecture, education, sport, law, taxi driving, carpet laying and more. Each job has its own challenges and pressures. These could be physical challenges like standing for long hours teaching or selling things in a shop, or finding how to stay relaxed while having to sit for long hours in an office or driving a car. They could be mental challenges, such as dealing with lots of critical feedback or feeling that you have to shoulder a lot of responsibility.

The ideas in this book can help on this journey of finding a quiet, flexible strength, which gives us a greater capacity to choose how we want to be in the world. If this intrigues you, this book is for you.

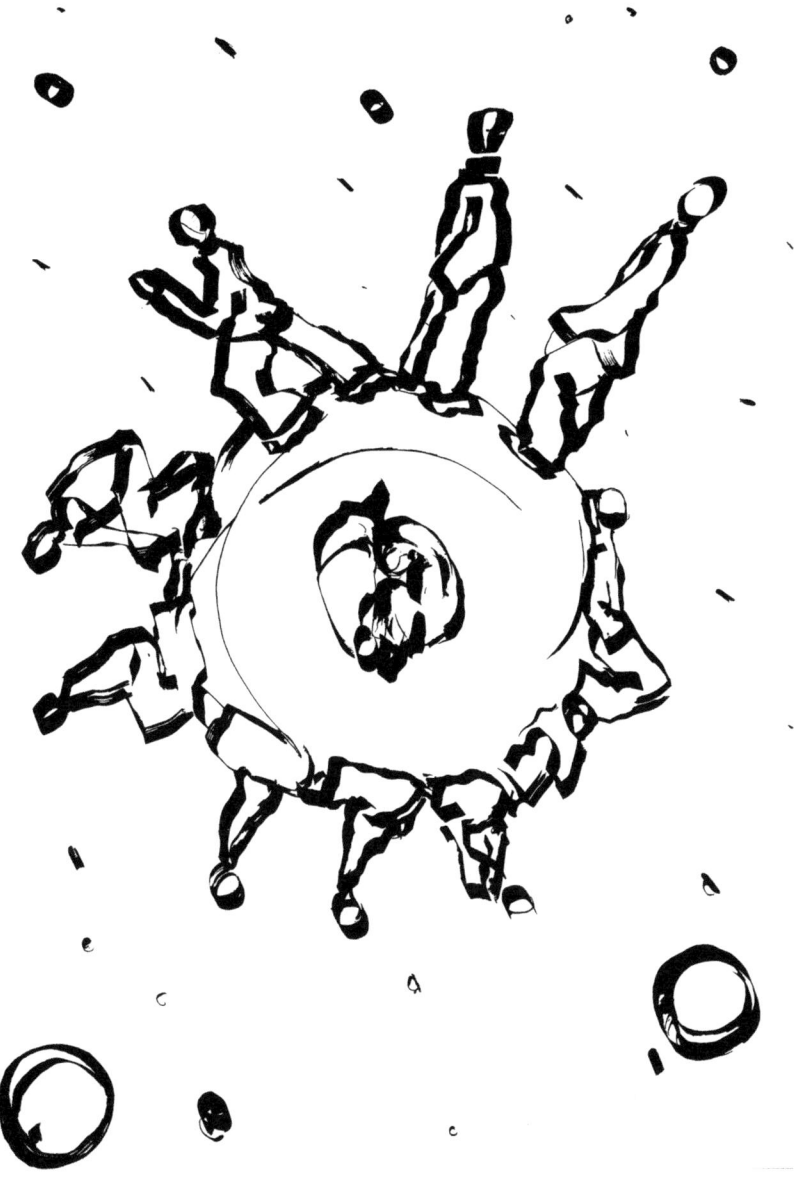

Introduction

Welcome to this book about taking steps on the journey of finding quiet strength even in great adversity. The drawings emerged from a lockdown project during the Covid-19 pandemic, when my family thought that if we couldn't see each other, we could post a creative thought on Instagram to stay in touch and keep cheerful. The pictures became a reminder of just how useful embodied skills are and how they have changed my life. These are important skills for connecting to ourselves, to each other and the world around us with more ease. During lockdown, many of us found that looking after ourselves and spending more time in nature re-established a deep link that we all have to our own human nature and wellbeing.

There is no quick fix to life, I expect we all wish there was. We all have to 'go through it' in terms of pain, grief, disappointments, anxieties and fears at some point – that's natural. It is good to know that there are practices that can help us find our resilience and buoyancy. Skills give us choices; imagine if we had all learnt the skills of emotional intelligence and embodied awareness at school: learnt to navigate the ups and downs, calmly and confidently, found out how to be present and aware of how we are doing what we are doing and learnt how to deal well with pressure and get over making mistakes and move on? It turns out that we can't tell ourselves how to feel but we can choose how to think, breathe and move differently and they affect how we feel. This, indirectly, makes all the difference. Sometimes we will need professional help (that's important), but we are also learning to look after our own mental, emotional and physical health for ourselves.

This book is a gentle start to building some skills of self-regulation and embodied resilience. It draws on well-researched and useful sources, sharing ideas and information in deliberately accessible, easy steps, so you don't have to sit on the top of a mountain for years to practise them. These experiments and practices will help us to stop and take a moment to notice our choices so that we can face and get through life's adversities, so we can find more hope for the future and more joy in being alive.

Choosing to be present and to connect changes us, especially if practised with the compassion of self-acceptance, curiosity, kindness and humour. If we look after ourselves and find our strength it's easier to hold our beliefs lightly, to find a way to be more peaceful with others and to take meaningful action for the world. If ever there was a time when we all need these qualities to help us stay as healthy as we can, to cope with change and take charge for the environment, it is now.

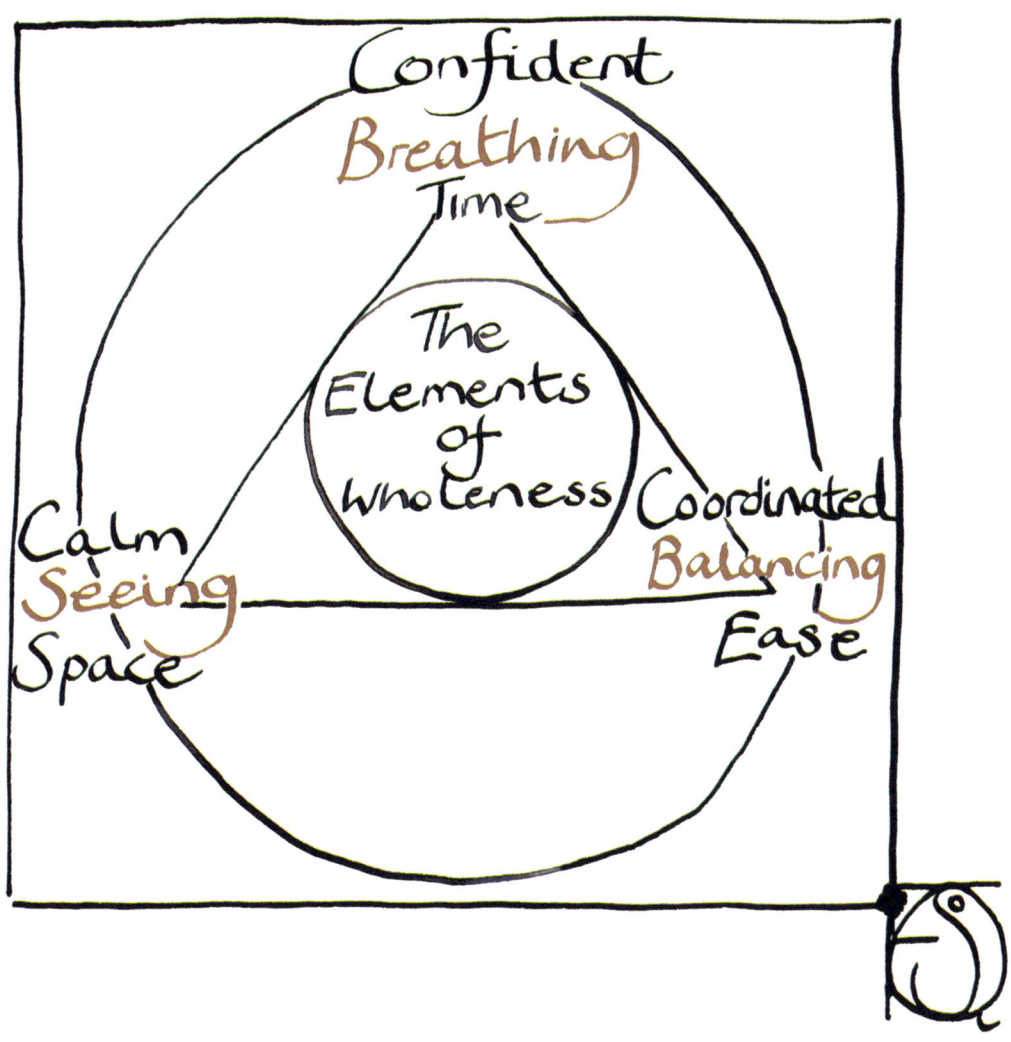

Finding quiet strength

A universal practical philosophy

Finding quiet strength tunes us into the practical philosophy of poise. It combines ancient wisdom and modern neuroscience, which tell us that we can be present in a way that develops both our emotional intelligence and embodied awareness and also helps us rediscover the balance of our lives. It is fundamental to the understanding of this work that we are all equal.

Whatever size, colour, race or creed, how we think, move and breathe makes much more difference to how we feel and relate to ourselves and each other than we might imagine. Having a practical philosophy to hang our hats on, to be able to rethink our habits, to choose to connect constructively to ourselves and each other, is a powerful way to rediscover a sense of quiet strength. This is about the personal becoming political, about learning to look after ourselves, each other and the planet.

Finding quiet strength

Finding quiet strength suggests resilience, without being overly stoic, showing compassion towards ourselves and others, especially when the chips are down. This allows us to find humour and lightness, as well as take things seriously when needed. This is all easier when we know how to organise and look after ourselves. If we don't know how to come back to finding a feeling of safety, we won't be able to think, act, move and breathe easily.

Finding

Finding is an ongoing practice rather than a search for a single answer, an easy curiosity, the sense of having a beginner's mind. Finding also implies the joy of discovery.

Quiet

Quiet implies a balance of our mind and body, finding a sense of calm and ease in our nervous system and its interconnection with our body, breath, muscles and structure.

Strength

Strength is being able to carry a great weight for a long time, but it also implies the strength of flexibility and fluidity – like a reed or a tree that moves easily in relationship to the wind, withstanding pressures while being rooted to the ground. Quiet strength is found in balance.

How to approach: integrating the elements of wholeness

We all feel at our best when we are in charge of our reactions and our choices. Identifying what we can influence is the first step. Understanding that we function as a whole, as a *psychophysical unity*, allows us to recognise the integration of the different elements of ourselves – our mind, body and emotions. This gives us more choices to connect and organise how we are reacting.

In order to identify elements of any skill we need to divide the skill up into component parts. But we also need to then bring those elements of that skill back together for it to work, rather like learning a language or a piece of music. In this book it is useful to bear in mind that we will be looking at different elements of the self in order to develop new skills but always come back to sensing these elements of self in the context of the whole.

Connecting, not correcting

The ideas in this book are about **connecting, not correcting**. It's easy to try to be perfect, slip into correcting our posture by trying to fix into an ideal position, or beat ourselves up about our mistakes, thoughts and feelings. This means we often give up before we have started because we have created a punitive relationship with our thoughts and bodies by telling ourselves off about feeling or looking a certain way. Here we are not trying to be perfect but to cultivate an attitude of choosing a calm, quiet confidence in connection to ourselves when we can – and when we can't, having a few useful strategies to help us reset. Trying used to mean experimenting, not 'trying hard'. Acknowledging making mistakes is usually how we learn. Finding how to approach change in this way is a quiet revolution.

The means whereby

It's not just what we do, it's how we do it. Rather than rushing to do everything and achieve it as quickly as possible – known as end-gaining – we can be interested and engaged in the process, the means whereby. We all know the cost of rushing an email or not taking time to bend freely when picking up something heavy. We stack up anxiety, make mistakes, become uncomfortable, hurt our backs, get grumpy. These become patterns of behaviour that put pressure on us and the people we love, make us lose our inner rhythm and our joy in everyday life. Taking a moment allows us to tune into rediscovering how to take our time and find space and ease in activity.

Just one thing

Rick Hanson, author of *Just One Thing*, talks about the importance of working with just one idea at a time, not tipping ourselves into cognitive overload. It is a bit like closing a few tabs on your browser. Working with one idea at a time lets us explore the consequences and effects of our ideas, letting them really land in our embodiment. We can grow these ideas slowly, see the effect on our mind, body and emotions, so that they become reliable short-term skills and a great pension plan too.

Inspired by nature

We are wired up to be connected not just to ourselves but also to each other, the space and the world around us. Developing this sense of spatial awareness helps us connect to the natural world and to be inspired by it. This can let us see parallels between ourselves and the natural world and in response enable us to change how we behave and interact within it. James Lovelock's Gaia Theory conceives of the Earth as an interconnected entity that includes all organisms within it. Learning to feel part of this global ecosystem, and comfortable within that, allows us to make choices with a sense of space in life, and a sense of being and acting as part of a sustainable whole.

Long game

Remember, a little thing done often makes a big difference over time. Think of these ideas and skills as part of the framework of how to be a human 'being'. Regularly choosing to be in touch with the whole of yourself, with your mind, body and emotions and understand how they integrate, are the first steps in looking after your long-term health and growing old gracefully with purpose. We gradually change thoughts and skills from short-term memory into our long-term embodied storage. I have added examples of useful books and ideas for further reading. Enquiring into ideas and having a repertoire of resources is an on-going way to look after our wellbeing.

Experiments in thought and movement

Alongside the ideas and information in this book are experiments in constructive thinking and movement, as well as ways to find a sense of wholeness. These are indicated by blue sections. The studies help us become aware of the component parts of everyday movement, then we can bring them back to a sense of flow. If any of the studies bring up overwhelming feelings it is important to seek competent professional help. When practicing these experiments it is good to stop, think and connect, take a moment to be present and stay attuned to yourself and the world around you. Take it slowly. This is the first experiment:

Finding Quiet Strength

One Step at a Time

Accept, acknowledge, allow

Stop – Come back to a quiet presence and notice what is going on.

Think – Tune into what you are doing now and how you are choosing to do it.

Connect – To your embodiment, your sense of grounding and safety, your breathing and to seeing the big picture of the room and the world around you.

Then **move on with ease**.

Calm

The embodied mind

Calm

The embodied mind

Having a calm mind gives us a more tranquil sense of embodiment and breath. Becoming aware of the habits of how we **think** and how our thoughts affect us and interact with our embodiment, breath and actions is fundamental to the practice of quiet strength. Our present habits might be old strategies that we thought or felt were useful at the time but now might need updating. Accepting ourselves as we are is the first step to self development.

We often have our own repetitive mental radio going on, so we normalise habits of anxious thoughts, almost like our own Greek chorus, and this can disconnect us from being present with our embodied reactions. This work is not about positive thinking but about what we can call *constructive thinking*; the thinking that opens us to a sense of wholeness. Finding our mind's interconnection with our embodiment can help us to reset to a quiet, calm sense of wholeness, to find our balance and poise. This quiet strength comes from being able to pause and listen, connect and regulate our whole self.

That we can **choose** to be present and notice what and how we think and connect is quite liberating. Requesting our mind to come to **quiet** gives us a wonderful little mental holiday, while we develop our **awareness** of what is going on in the present moment. Ongoing anxiety that lies below our radar – at a subconscious level – might be more in the driving seat of our everyday lives than we thought. Our conscious mind might not yet have registered the embodied signals of fear, worry or anger. What is surprising is that once we tune into these signals we wonder how the jeepers we missed them before – rather like suddenly noticing that we are hungry or tired or need to go to the loo. Instead of just letting them organise our behaviour in the background, we can begin to be able to regulate back to a quieter calm and ease and a sense of safety.

Hearing these embodied signals, we begin to have more agency in the sequence and rhythms of our reactions. This means we can not only choose to regulate ourselves but notice how we co-regulate with others too. It really does seem like re-tuning a radio into clarity. We start to hear the early

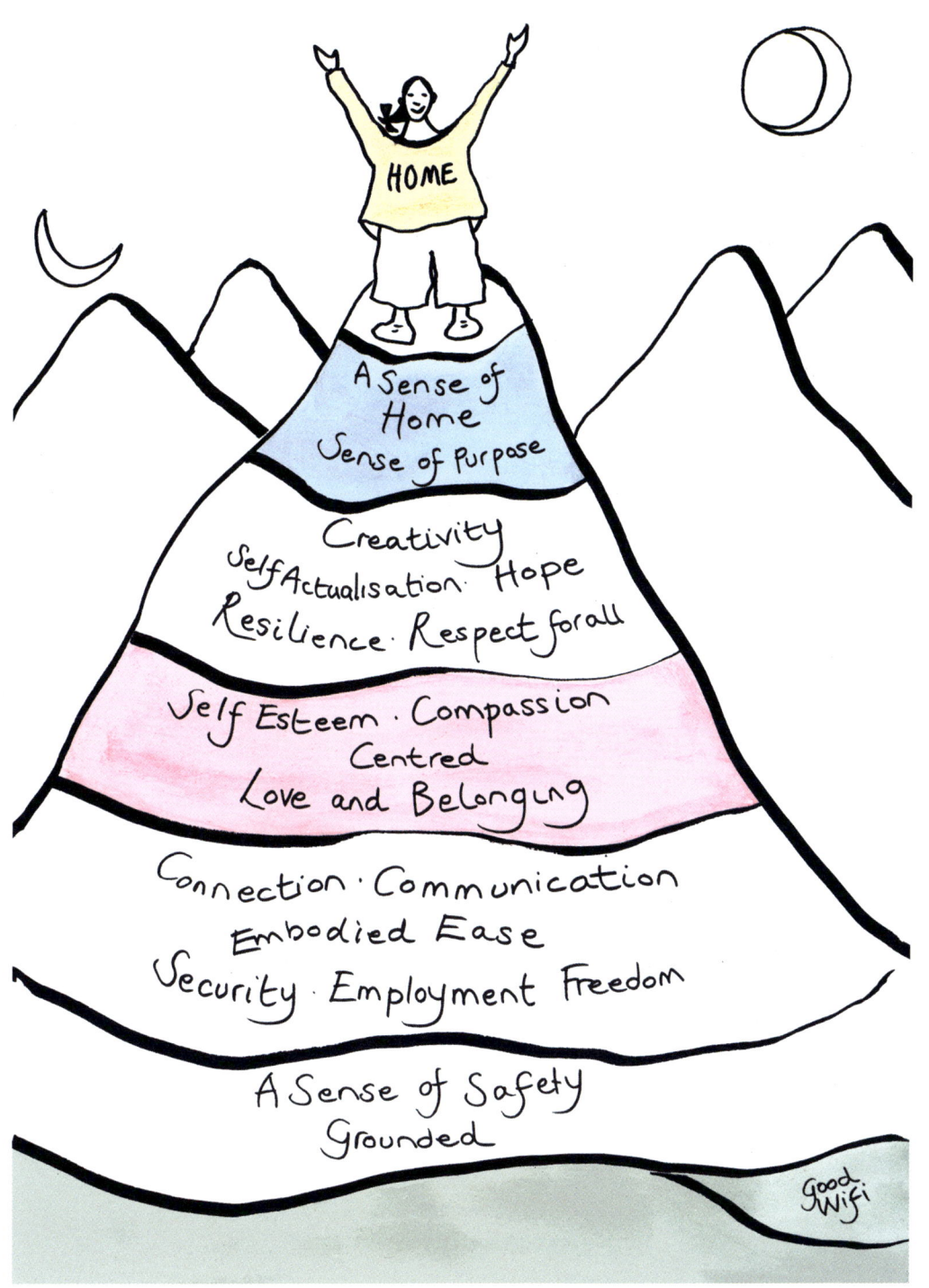

Maslow's Hierarchy of Needs

Finding a Quiet Mind and an Easy Body

underlying messages of turbulence and defence, the sense of not being heard, or anger at not getting our own way. When we hear these signals, it is time to redial, to breathe, to look out, to release by grounding, and let go of getting smaller. Getting smaller means pulling our bodies inwards – for example, pulling our heads down, our shoulders up and in, and holding our breath or tensing our stomach muscles.

These ideas may sound simple but when we are under pressure they can be elusive, so it's good to practise them and make them more readily available. Where to start? By noticing that taking a moment is a skill we already have and can develop. When we pause and take a moment we give ourselves a chance to consciously choose to tune into what is going on, then we can choose to redirect our thoughts. This also helps us notice when our mind wanders and chatters and when we lose track of an easy concentration on what we are doing.

Cultivating a quiet mind and an easy body

Hope is at hand. When we are more able to recognise the embodiment of our mental and emotional state and what triggers these patterns, we can regulate earlier and more easily, even when we are under great stress.

Let's start by stopping.

The practice of presence begins with the skill of pausing our mental dialogue, being present in our mind and in our body, taking a moment to breathe and ask our mind to return to a state of quiet and our body to a state of ease. In the process it helps to release our linguistic muscles and structures, including our tongue, jaw, face and even our throat. Mental chatter (and anxiety) can often keep these muscles busy and tense, even if we are not speaking out loud. The skill of pausing and finding a quiet mind can be practised in the garden, up a mountain, on the bus or on the tube. Once we are able to pause, we can then weave this quiet ease into our day.

Relaxing the mind

1. Sit comfortably now. The aim of this practice is to take ten quiet breaths; see if you can slightly extend the out breath, peacefully pause, then let the in breath be free and easy. If you get distracted it can help to gently hold each finger with your other hand in turn as a reminder to stay with the ten breaths while developing ease.

2. Each time you breathe, see if you can release your linguistic muscles – your tongue, face and jaw– as this will help you let go of memories and prevent future planning crashing in. If thoughts do come, let them pass – rather like a wave, or a bus, or a cloud – and let yourself return to quiet or gently say to the thoughts, 'Not now. I will look after you later'.

3. Once you have done this, try doing the same thing with five breaths, three breaths, then just one breath. Notice that, with practice, you might only need one breath to reset to ease.

We are finding the practice of presence, the power of now.

How we embody emotion

We naturally react to immediate threats with the startle pattern. Historically, this was to keep us safe. The startle reaction triggers the nervous system's patterns of fight, flight or freeze. It's appropriate under certain conditions to have the energy of these fear reactions, such as in an accident or when under immediate serious threat to life, but not so great to be stuck in them chronically all day, every day.

It is through messages from our senses that our brain perceives whether we are under threat or not, though this might be at a subconscious level. Our brain passes on these messages to our autonomic nervous system, which organises the constantly changing balance and tempo of our inner organs, regulating our heartbeat, breath and digestion.

The autonomic nervous system divides into the sympathetic and parasympathetic. The sympathetic nervous system triggers the fight-or-flight response when we are under threat. It is often thought of as the mobilisation system, as we get a surge of energy while our hearts are pounding from the chemistry of adrenaline and cortisol. The parasympathetic nervous system, on the other hand, calms everything down and takes us towards the so-called rest-and-digest response when we begin to feel less fearful. When we have been overwhelmed by trauma or stress for a long time, our parasympathetic nervous system can react by immobilising us and causing a great loss of energy. These historical patterns of fear can also be triggered and held by responses to modern life's mental and emotional threats.

Structurally, we can carry on holding gestures of fight, flight or freeze when we are not actually under immediate threat, even when we are just writing an email or watching TV. We can hold on to tension, fixing into a slight flinch or a lifted, tight chest that can lead to pain and discomfort. If we continue to do this we shorten and narrow – literally getting smaller, tighter, stiffer and even holding our breath as we assimilate these patterns and emotions into our body.

When we are upset, tired or overwhelmed, flexor muscles tend to come into play with the effect being that we can become physically heavy. These can become long-held habits and gestures of collapsing. If we can let go of the flexor muscles and restore the strength and ease in our extensor muscles,

our spine will lengthen and our back will be wide and free. By counteracting these different habits and fear reflexes, which can become normalised in our body, indirectly we can find an inner calm, clarity and courage.

What we are interested in is the ability to identify and regulate these reactions back to safety and an easy energy and how to quieten ourselves back to a balanced place of tranquillity. At other times, if we have become fixed, depressed or very low in energy and mood, we will want to know how to rev up our energy a little to become alert and ready for activity. Rather than just being in those emotional energy states, we can understand and recognise them in an embodied way. This means we will be more able to notice and regulate our embodied feelings, recognise our needs that can be met with respect, kindness and compassion and negotiate with other people's needs and feelings in the same way. It is useful to be quite specific about what you are feeling emotionally so that you can understand it, then put it into the context of the bigger embodied picture.

Moments of perceived threat in our modern everyday lives can set in motion these ancient patterns of anxiety and startle. For example, if we experience a sudden loss of confidence or a sense of being judged, it can make us feel smaller, hold our breath and lose a sense of the space around us. Being upset can trigger anger and fight, and when we are trapped in these patterns of startle, we are less able to cope with life's ups and downs and we find it harder to reset to ease. If we are disconnected from our bodies, we are also disconnected from the useful information that can help us regulate back to safety. Conscious compassionate attention can befriend our subconscious memories, fears and habits. We can bring our kind intention to gentle change that is long lasting and sustained.

A great source of further information about understanding and befriending our autonomic nervous system (through the Polyvagal theory, a term developed by Stephen Porges), is Deb Dana's book, *Anchored*.

Take a moment to be in the moment

Sit comfortably and consider letting yourself be as safe as you possibly can be in this moment. Let yourself think of being soft and tall, free and easy as you are quietly present.

Memory and emotion

Stored within us are the memories of our life and all that has happened. If we have had tricky experiences and did not process them, these memories will live in the emotional part of our brain, in our muscles and our viscera, and will deeply affect the way we feel, move and breathe. A heavy burden that we carry over the long term can be our destructive memories that can become embodied. Just think of getting a piece of good or bad news, in that moment our embodiment changes. Sometimes we will need help with unravelling these cares and woes. This is a moment to ask for support.

To be able to release and return to an easier pattern of moving and breathing not only helps us feel better in the present, but it also helps us move on from the past. It is important to avoid getting smaller. It's not that we want to get bigger, as that is rather like the fight mode, but to have the confidence to take up our space and move and breathe freely and easily in activity. When we learn not to hold onto these embodied red lights of danger, fight-or-flight, or the amber lights of defence, fix-or-freeze, we can release into a sense of freedom and poise. We can then find flow in activity and an easy interaction with our friends and colleagues.

Our embodied ease supports our mindset, and vice versa. Regulating back to centre and ease takes practice but this is what our modern brain can do.

The Journey of our Nervous System

We can learn to recognise emergency signals and introduce a sense of safety. Immediate signals of threat can be balanced regularly with a more everyday sense of embodied ease and vitality. It's great to have a repertoire of thoughts and activities that help plug you back into feelings of belonging, significance, being valued and cherished, and really absorbing them, so you are not getting smaller but getting easier. We can begin to befriend ourselves.

Trauma

Most of us will have had the experience of some trauma in our lives, which will sit deeply in our heart, mind and body. Unpacking the embodiments of trauma – the patterns of tension which are unresolved – can be so useful, as it means we can rewire our thoughts because the body and mind are always interacting. There is much more understanding these days of the role of trauma in people's everyday lives and it is important to address this if you begin to identify deeply held worries, memories and anxieties. Talking therapies also recognise the importance of not just how we think but also how we embody these thoughts.

Being present with the whole of ourselves can sometimes be painful when we have a lot to deal with. The pulls of our attention to the past or the future often mean we miss the good – the **sense** of being present and alive. Gradually, when we find a quiet acceptance of the past and some optimism for the future, it is easier to have a sense of being here in the now.

Understanding the connections our nervous system makes to our body helps us understand the patterns of tension and find ways to release them.

A hugely important regulator of our nervous system is the vagus nerve. Known as the wanderer, it travels all the way from our head, face and mouth via the throat and heart to our guts and abdomen. Integrating release in these three areas helps us be in touch with and regulate the vagus nerve. We might need to unpack these three areas one at a time, then let them integrate into an easy sense of wholeness. Allowing these areas to come together like a chord of notes chiming simultaneously can make a big difference to our sense of safety. Noticing these releases of our inner tension and the tempo of our breath lets us hear the conversation between our inner movement and our outer structure. Sometimes we are fixing and constricting this interaction. The good news is we can learn to let go.

A helpful book for further reading on healing trauma is *Waking the Tiger* by Peter Levine.

Releasing exercise

1 Put your hands on the nape of your neck and stroke around your neck, across your shoulders and down the length of the front of your torso.

2 See if you can let go of tension in your face, mouth and neck. Notice if you are pressing your tongue to the roof of your mouth. Instead, lightly engage the tip of your tongue behind the top teeth, allowing your mouth to be wet. Let your face muscles be easy. Notice letting the root of your tongue release and allow your throat, neck and face to be free.

3 Allow yourself to integrate your awareness of these freedoms of the face, mouth and neck, with an ease in your chest and shoulder area as you breathe gently.

4 See if you can include being aware of your breath and the way it can influence a release in your lower belly and solar plexus too. Try it and see if you can gently slow your breathing down by slightly lengthening the outbreath, which connects us to the parasympathetic nervous system (see page 24).

5 Notice the integration of freedom in these three areas as you breathe, letting this help you feel safe and connected in the present.

We can find safety

Recognising what triggers our reactions is very useful. Our brain has a negativity bias; this strategy originated to keep us safe, but now we are less at risk of getting eaten it is not always useful. We can become aware of what triggers our emotions, both negatively and positively, so we can transform feelings of being under threat and regulate back into a sense of safety.

There are many life changes that put us under pressure, and that is understandable. Learning to be onside with yourself about ageing, grief, moving house, ill health, worrying for others is very important. Change of any sort – even positive change – can be hard, but there will always be change. Getting through tricky situations can take time. Humans do get sad and feel overwhelmed, we all do. We need to learn to process these changes and sometimes we need extra help. The good news is we can reorganise our embodied thinking and manage our emotions, let water flow under the bridge. When we give ourselves time, we can choose how we might approach triggers and reaction patterns, then process our emotions and learn to initiate an embodied sense of safety and create safe boundaries.

Choosing how to give feedback to yourself about your reactions is a skill that is worth developing. We often slip back into old patterns: historic resonances, the habits of blame and being negative towards ourselves and others. More usefully, we can learn to be able to give ourselves **constructive feedback** rather than only negative feedback. This is inclusive of the understanding, 'if I think, breathe and move like this, I will feel like that'.

Maybe we will need to change our perception and not think life is going to be perfect, but will need navigation and that is a skill we can develop. Noticing how integrated our thoughts are with our emotions and with our embodiment is a deeper way of noticing being alive.

Stop, think and connect

1. Notice which thoughts and feelings make you hold your breath, fix your body and get smaller. Give yourself a moment. Choose to be present.

2. Breathe. Notice which thoughts help return you to find the conditions of ease, safety and alert calmness.

Identifying emotions

A very useful skill to develop is *mentalising*. This is the ability to notice and label what you are thinking and its effect on your feelings. This can include noticing the tone in which you are thinking as well as the noise and tempo of your thoughts. This might sound easy and obvious but very often we are just feeling the feeling and not recognising the thought that we are embodying. By recognising this thought we can acknowledge the feeling – is it hurt, anger, grief, betrayal, fear? Sometimes we might just need to sit with the thoughts and feelings for a while to unpack them and what they are actually telling us. Be more specific with what you are feeling. The more accurately you can identify the emotion, the more you can notice its connection with your thoughts.

There are no wrong emotions. Noticing how we are embodying thoughts as feelings is important if we want to be able to regulate them. This can be helped by noticing the loop between the muscle tension, gestures and our feelings that we might not have realised were there, such as frowning, tightening our mouths or holding our stomach muscles. These tensions can trap the thoughts and feelings rather than let us gradually process and work through them. Identifying how dysregulated emotions can disconnect us from being present, grounded and centred, is something that can change as we develop our awareness.

Noticing feelings that might be unmet, or unidentified needs from the past, is incredibly helpful. We can identify what we need: to feel more heard, chat something through, or maybe we just need to get more rest and sleep to find our inner resilience. When we are able to choose to be present, safe, grounded and connected this can take the edge off painful thoughts and feelings. However, it is very, very important to recognise that sometimes we need a chat with a friend, a bit of a moan or a big old cry, and sometimes we need more professional help. It's important to figure out what we need and when.

Finding your emotional toolkit

1. See if you can identify the challenge or the stimulus that has created your emotional reaction.

2. See if you can sit quietly and unpack what you are feeling, being very specific.

3. Notice if you can draw on some of your life skills of patience and resilience to address the situation.

4. Remember you are growing your toolkit of useful thoughts and skills to put these life skills in place.

5. For example this could be finding your quiet mind and easy body. Remember you are finding your emotional intelligence, your embodied awareness to deal with situations that put you under pressure.

What we can choose to change?

Giving ourselves the choice of what to pay attention to and how we think is our big choice in life. One of our greatest freedoms is to be able to choose how we react. One of the main aims of this book is to encourage us to realise we have choices. We can begin to include choices about how we think, breathe and move in our everyday, so we can find equanimity.

Norman Doidge, in *The Brain that Changes Itself*, writes about how we can rewire our brain, how our brain is plastic, and how we can change the patterns through conscious choices of thought and imagination.

The understanding of neuroplasticity is that 'neurons that fire together wire together'. In other words, we can change our habits by thinking new thoughts. Hearing our thought patterns in a kind way and noticing how we embody them, empowers us to regulate them. Having clear intensions with our thoughts can make a big difference. Remembering to listen to ourselves compassionately but clearly, like a dear friend would.

Connecting to release, releasing to connect

1. Place your right hand under your left arm pit (near your heart), and your left hand on your right shoulder or upper arm, noticing the movement of your breath and the touch kindly containing you. Let yourself stay with this for a moment or two.

2. Sense you are soothing yourself, a little like giving yourself a kind and friendly hug.

Absorbing the good

Being present and able to absorb quiet and calm experiences deeply in ourselves means we can balance our energies and tempo, find ease and be able to rest and sleep. Some of us do love the energy of scary movies, too many coffees, rollercoasters and adversarial arguments and while this isn't wrong, of course, it's good to have balance and not be in a continual state of anxiety. We often don't make wise choices when we are in an anxious state because our reactions can be too fast – rather like pressing send before you have checked which name you put in the address box! Finding ways to reprogramme ourselves to absorb the good in quiet everyday pleasures and experiences brings more health, tranquillity and joy into our lives.

Absorbing the good, the ease of things that make us happy, calm and joyful and really taking time to savour them and recognise them helps to balance our nervous systems back to calm. This can help with long-term and long-held anxieties, as well as short-term disturbances. This means we are not only transforming negative states but consciously cultivating positive states – rather like a farmer getting in the winter stores during the summer. Looking after ourselves is such an important skill. It's not a selfish thing, it's like putting on your own oxygen mask first on a plane.

Learning to look after ourselves

1. Pause and let yourself be present.

2. Remember a place that you really enjoy being in.

3. Think of someone who loves you unconditionally.

4. Remember a moment that makes you smile, a time that you really enjoyed with friends, or perhaps being at a concert. Take a few deeper breaths in and longer breaths out to come back to the present.

5. Think of an activity you have really enjoyed; it can be something very simple.

6. Let yourself stay with the good sense of these thoughts for longer, let them land and allow yourself to really absorb them for a few seconds. Imagine this creating a balance of energies within you.

7. Absorb the thoughts – you can even press your thumb and middle finger together to feel like you are embodying this process.

The three questions

There are three questions that simplify putting the conditions of safety, ease and readiness in place. We can think of this as our 'ready list'. Before we go into an activity, asking these questions allows us to become present. The three questions create the sense we have when we are on a beach or a mountaintop. We feel ready for anything. Our eyes are relaxed, we breathe freely and feel a sense of balance and embodiment. This reminds us to be open to joy, contentment and hope.

The ready list

A good way to be present is to stop, pause and ask yourself three questions:

1. **Are you seeing?** Are you seeing the big picture or are you overfocused on your screen?

2. **Are you breathing?** Which really means, are you holding on to getting smaller or one aspect of the breath cycle?

3. **Are you balanced?** Are you standing with your weight balanced between your two feet, feeling soft and tall, free and easy up through your body?

Giving ourselves little moments to stop, think and connect – to see, breathe and balance – can make all the difference and we can weave this into our day.

Open mind

'The mind is like a parachute – it works best when it's open.' We all need a sense of safety, but at the same time we can open our minds to change and the new. This can allow us to be free to explore and learn and find our beginner's mind. Perhaps another sign of an open mind is being able to hear something new, or someone else's point of view, calmly, without getting too impatient or cross. To be ready to try out a new experience happily we need to feel ready. Sometimes the unknown is tricky to negotiate, but a great phrase created by a friend, Family Therapist Barry Mason, is *safe uncertainty*. This is a state of tuning into biological ease where we remind ourselves to be **safe**, to feel at home with ourselves, so we can interact well with others while also dealing well with change and be open to new experiences and changing our mind, bringing a new outlook to our lives.

Calm

Knowing and trusting that we can return to this state of calm curiosity means we will be interested in lifelong learning. We all get cabin fever when we stay at home all the time, as we know from the past years of lockdowns, or we can get anxious at the thought of change, new experiences and going out again. We need to safely expand our comfort zones, but safety doesn't need to be sameness. New experiences don't have to be epic; they can be gentle and rewarding and include cultivating friendships and taking time to explore our environment.

Everyday joys can include seeing, breathing and balancing, and the great news is these are free. Absorbing the benefit of just being present in the everyday is what can make a difference to letting go of anxious thought patterns and feeling overwhelmed and pressured by our lives.

We can underestimate the value of taking a moment, but we often see people in peak-performance situations pausing, taking time to breathe out, to compose themselves and absorb a sense of readiness to ease themselves into the next new challenge. We need to weave this into our everyday, to prevent anxiety patterns building up so that we can trust that we will then deal well with new experiences, bigger problems because we know how to find ease. We see this in the animal kingdom, as a creature with embodied intelligence takes a moment before springing into action with grace and ease.

Expand into your comfort zone

1. Identify new experiences that you enjoyed and remember that when you are not overtired or upset you might be more ready to open up to the new, including new opinions.

2. Notice registering new things even in your everyday environment: new views, new routes.

3. Be open to pictures you forget to look at, windows we forget to see out of. Remember, you do know how to be open and easy when you feel safe.

4. Avoid holding your breath; breathe in and out freely, especially if you feel a bit wobbly.

Finding time, space and ease

Developing our embodied awareness gives us more choices to notice signs of anxiety as well as recognise when we are comfortable and happy and acknowledge the integration of signals in our body and mind. The habits of mental chatter and worry usually mean our inner tempo feels faster: our tongue gets pressed to the roof of our mouth, our jaw gets tight, our teeth clench, our facial muscles grip, our eyes frown, our shoulders narrow and our neck and throat tighten. What a lot of energy we can waste. This awareness gives us a chance to choose to give up these habits of tension when we are ready. It is just like pausing at the red light to avoid oncoming traffic or counting to ten – skills that we have already, we are just refining them. We can then develop these skills of stopping and noticing in activity, slowing that rushing, impatient feeling and beginning to negotiate our energy. Letting go of the rush means we can find ease, safety and readiness for activity. Then we can enjoy the sense of having time, space and ease and we can reconnect to the world.

Choosing to stop and reconnect with embodied calm when we can makes a big difference when we make other choices, such as what to eat, when to take breaks, what to buy and what not to buy, as well as how to choose, over and again, to look after ourselves. When we find the 'means-whereby' to look after ourselves, and to create new and skilful habits, to enjoy the process, it is easier to help the world and other people.

Creating time, space and ease

1 Can you stop, think and connect to slow down your inner tempo to give yourself time? This is usually helped not only by slowing down our movement and pace but also by our breathing rate, too.

2 Can you find your grounding – give up getting smaller and tune into being open in relation to the full volume of your body – and notice and see the space around you as well?

3 Can you be easy, not fixed or held? Can you come to quiet and give up continuously chatting in your mind? Being easy and ready usually feels like being balanced and poised.

4 Can you let yourself release a sense of rush and worry and instead allow yourself to feel centred and calm?

5 Can you ask yourself the three questions, am I seeing, breathing and balancing?

Semi-supine

A wonderful practice for constructive rest is to lie down in semi-supine. It's like putting in a break, giving ourselves a little a holiday, stepping off the hamster wheel, letting go of cognitive overload! It's interesting to see children often lie down like this naturally, as do animals, re-finding a sense of deep time and deep space. There are many benefits to this active rest; it puts us in a good relationship with gravity, and it also lets our spines find their natural length and our backs to find their natural width. We can then take this ease into our day. This practice can develop into active rest but can also just give us a moment to find our human **being**. Sometimes it's good to stop trying to figure it all out.

How to restore equilibrium

Lie down on your back on a firm but soft surface. Have your knees bent up, feet on the floor, and let your arms be either by your side or place your hands on your tummy, with a book under your head to support your head and neck. It can be lovely to close your eyes for a while and rest.

Confidence

Structure and breath

Confidence

Structure, Breath and Emotion
When we lose our structural integrity things can start to become uncomfortable, we can lose our confidence and balance. We wouldn't expect a building to have unstable foundations or a table to work well when it wasn't balanced, so it's surprising how easy it is to ignore the balance and easy alignment of our structure and its integration with our sense of self. A good understanding of structure is 'there's no right position but only the right condition'.

Stability and elasticity
Our structure has a method to its madness; seemingly unstable and easy to collapse or become fixed, we are actually beautifully evolved to be strong, aligned, grounded and light, to balance, bend and stretch with ease. This is all much more possible and available if we understand how to find our poise and equilibrium. We weren't taught that how we sit, stand and walk are all fundamental to our physical and mental health, but they are. We embody our confidence, humour and dignity both to ourselves and others when we allow ourselves to find our poise.

Often, we lose structural integrity not just from sitting down for too long but from feelings of being under pressure, being undermined, overwhelmed, overthinking, overscheduled or just criticised by ourselves and others. It is then that our body starts to collapse and become rigid or tense and restless under pressure. It is useful to remember that what might have become our normal isn't actually natural. When we feel comfortable, curious and our energy is not exhausted or overexcited, we can find the quiet strength and ease of our structure through balancing the qualities of strength, flexibility, fluidity and elasticity needed for the activity we are doing.

We often imagine that spending time at the gym here and there or going for the odd walk or run will reset us to structural balance, but it makes more sense that our overall ease will be developed in our everyday lives, by knowing how to sit, stand, walk and run freely with poise. We will save the NHS hours of time and money if we educate ourselves to find our natural harmony in everyday movement.

Confidence

Rethinking our posture as a **condition** of ease, poise and balance rather than a **position** can be life-changing. We can think of being dynamic in our stillness and free in our movement. There is no such thing as a fixed state of balance, it is more useful to think of rebalancing as an ongoing process. Imagine stillness more as a state of quiet equilibrium.

The sense of pain

We tend to celebrate long hours, overworking and material success above ease. If we have got to the stage of being in pain it is definitely time to stop and change something. Pain is a red light.

Pain signals that it's time to take notice of what is going on; it is caused not only by accidents and illness but by the way we use ourselves in everyday life, the choices we make on a day-to-day basis of how we sit, stand, walk, clean the dishes, vacuum the floor, put the rubbish out or do the gardening.

Chronic physical and emotional pain are hard to bear. We know from research that more of us suffer from back pain, migraines and jaw ache at an earlier age and in greater numbers than ever before. Today, back pain is estimated to affect 60–70 per cent of adults in industrialised countries. In our modern, sedentary society these are genuine risks for everyone.

Small everyday choices to bring our intelligence to how we are sitting and standing can be the pathway to ease. When we make the link between physical balance, mental equilibrium and the overall balance of our lives, it becomes easier to see patterns and 'sets' that cause us pain.

There are lots of everyday remedies that can help – ice on immediate pain, heat on long-term pain and regular resting in semi-supine position (see page 40) is a great way to address back pain. Have a think about what you do regularly, how you sit at your computer and for how long. Bring your intelligence to sitting well, being grounded and in balance and how you move in your everyday life.

Physical pain can be the manifestation of mental suffering; we see this in a dramatic way if we witness someone having a panic attack. Today, there is more mental anguish and anxiety especially among young people than ever before. Seeing the interplay between our 'mindset' and our 'body set' – the way we use ourselves – is key to being able to release habits that create pain. We begin to understand this loop of interaction between the pain in our mind, body and emotions. It might just be time to stop and rest in semi-supine.

Variables

Rather than thinking about tension as good or bad, a useful way to consider it is as one of the many variables that are part of being human.

Try thinking about the tension in your body on a scale of zero to ten. With zero tension it feels comfortable for a while, but notice how we lose all sense of structure and form and any sense of energy. This is perfect for sleeping when we are supported and horizontal. If you are constantly in a ten state of

tension, zero might be a very appealing option, but thinking of ten, or any other degree of tension, as wrong would be a shame. However, while ten could be perfect in a life-threatening situation it is unsustainable all the time; it starts to affect other variables, like our breathing, our digestion and sense of wellbeing.

Experimenting with variables

1. Try thinking of being in a ten state, feeling as much tension as you can find; notice how we lose a sense of grounding and width, and lift up.

2. Try sitting or standing, or any movement, in a zero state of tension and then again try a ten state. I'm guessing you will find that neither of them are great for long periods.

3. Experiment now with releasing into a five state, where you have a sense of height and width, as well as an easy sense of structure and volume. You might also find a calm energy and a readiness to move more freely.

Variables

Letting our chatting brain have a question to think about that is non-judgemental can be useful. Just asking ourselves what state we are in is a useful question; we can then regulate up and down the scale. With our skill of seeing, breathing and balancing it is easier to come back to this five state. When we are in control of tension as a variable, we are much more likely to find our inner strength and resilience to cope with everyday challenges.

This idea of variables on a scale can be applied to any aspect of how we use our body. For example, we could imagine our energy levels on a one-to-ten scale or see only a small, focused area versus having a panoramic awareness, breathing shallowly or deeply. The list of variables could go on; the important thing is the non-judgemental curiosity. This technique for noticing what we are paying attention to and how, is drawn from *The Inner Game* by Timothey Gallwey, a useful resource for learning any skill.

Confidence

Can it be easier?

What would this activity be like or look like if it was easier? Allowing this thought to give us a choice helps us register if we are in a 'trying hard' mindset, which can lead to pain. Notice activities that put you under pressure, when you feel in a rush, tense, your body feels fixed – you stop breathing freely, clench your toes, narrow your shoulders. This can build up if, for example, we stay seated at our computers for a long time.

Effort can include not just the tension we have but also the heavy downwards pull we can embody. Are you under pressure when you sit for a long time? Inactivity can be as difficult for our embodiment as anything. Thinking of sitting or standing in a more active way and being in an easy condition of balance and lightness is very helpful. Thinking 'Can it be easier?' may encompass letting go of tension, fixing, heaviness or rushing.

Letting go

It takes an awful lot of letting go to actually drop things. When we begin to notice how much extra effort we are putting into holding onto things such as toothbrushes, cups or pens, we can reduce this. Notice how much freer you feel when you use less effort.

1. Try lifting your lower arms with as little effort as possible.

2. Try picking something up with as little effort as possible.

Many traditions talk about this 'being easier' (sometimes known as non-doing) from Zen to mindfulness. When we don't approach activity with any preconceived habitual effort of how the activity goes, we can find the appropriate tension. There are places in the body where we tend to hold the tension of trying hard, shoulders and necks for example.

Non-doing is not doing nothing. Non-doing is thinking, being or moving with ease and grace, avoiding striving or trying too hard. It is the opposite of end-gaining, where one focuses on completing the goal rather than the process of the task in hand. Applying non-doing to our embodiment, movement and breath is wonderful, giving up trying hard to be right or careful, just allowing a sense of enjoying being easy in activity.

Confidence

Stop, think, connect: coming back to quiet

Our embodied habits are usually caused by pressure of time in a particular activity. A great way to change these habits is by building space before the activity to give yourself a moment to stop, think and connect. Then you can let your awareness and ease flow through into the activity.

Thinking in activity

Stop for a moment to come back to quiet, notice how you embody your reaction to an activity, for example washing up. Can it be easier? Associate stopping with being present and breathing out. Weaving these moments of deeper choice and awareness through the day so whatever you are doing can become easier and more enjoyable.

Cultivating a sense of direction, from thought connecting to embodied calm, can take a moment to land. It is good to renegotiate this sort of connection on a regular basis because, as we know, old habits can linger. Again, it is important not to try too hard. It turns out we can't try hard to be free! Just enjoy the thought of being in touch with your whole self in a gentle way. There are no wrong or right positions, but there are certainly more or less easy conditions.

Connect and direct

The three questions (see page 36) allow us to find calm and ease and we can go on to develop these connections and directions. Directions allow you to connect to your embodiment, to sense and move in a new way, taking your quiet intention into your body. They recalibrate your body, breath and movement, so you can be lighter, easier and freer. Experiment now with taking your calm, conscious thoughts into directing and connecting with your body. Notice when we stop pulling down, we go up.

1. Register your feet on the ground, connect to your body sense.

2. Send a direction through your whole body: think of being soft and tall, your back and shoulders being wide and free. Avoid lifting, let these thoughts be easy.

3. Think of letting your neck be free and allow your head to release up into balance. We will be calling this freedom in the relationship between our head and our body our primary freedom, as it facilitates a global freedom in our body.

Enjoy connecting to how you feel when you are calm, confident and coordinated.

Confidence

Composing ourselves

Stopping, thinking and connecting helps us to compose ourselves. Developing our sense of tuning in and directing connects us to being present and awake. This listening in stillness can become gently active, by listening to the quality of how we are doing an activity rather than just doing it. A request rather than an order to be alert. Directions help us avoid getting smaller or trying hard to be bigger than we are. If we have a good body map, we can direct our thoughts and energy subtly to where we need to release unnecessary tension. The subtle free movement of directions releases us so that we stay in touch with balance, volume and ease. This is as simple as imagining your body has asked for directions. Your job is to allow yourself to release into them, not to try hard to go there. If we direct our body like this, we avoid pushing or pulling or trying to get the right position. Instead, we can stay relaxed, sensing a condition of ease. We are thinking of being released rather than relaxed and collapsed. Trusting that change will happen and quiet poised energy will develop with practice.

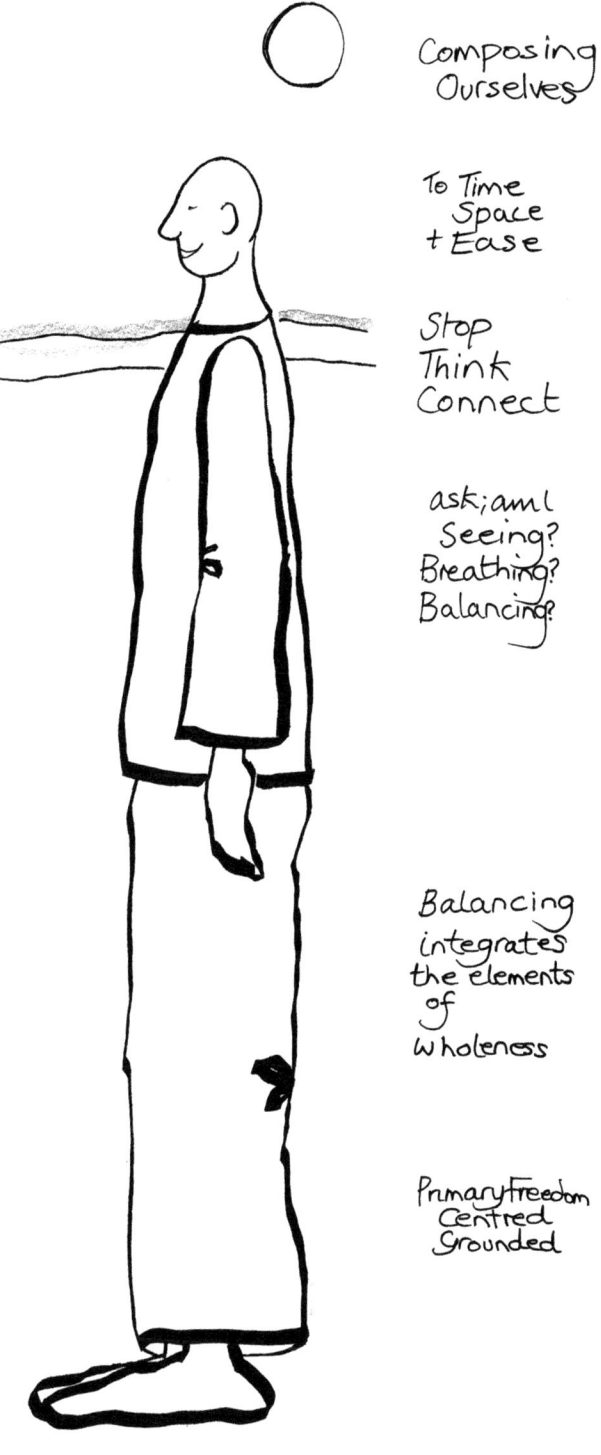

Rejoining the present

1. Take a simple activity you do everyday when you can give yourself a little full-stop moment, a breath, before carrying on. This could be opening your computer or brushing your teeth. We can give ourselves an intention to enjoy these everyday activities – we don't need to get happy-clappy about it, just be present and easy.

2. Can we slow down the activity? Sometimes it's really nice just to hear the water running into the sink or feel the sun coming in through the window.

Building a repertoire of constructive language to connect

It's interesting how much our nervous system responds to words; just one word or phrase can change the day. Creating a little library of words, useful questions and phrases that help us connect, can be very reassuring. For example: **Stop, think, connect** to give yourself **time, space and ease** by asking the questions: **Am I seeing? Am I breathing? Am I balancing?**

The integration of balance with the elements of wholeness

1. Notice first that you're grounded through your contact points.

2. Now integrate a sense of the next layer up of ease, your centre. Release your lower belly, let it be free to move and breathe.

3. Now include thinking that your head, neck and shoulders are light, your upper torso is free and integrated with your soft, tall spine, available to easy movement.

4. Enjoy opening your vision into the panoramic, let yourself sense the whole of you in volume, free to move and available to easy breathing.

5. Sense that you are grounded, centred, soft, tall and aware of the space around you. Let these sensations integrate into a sense of wholeness, like different elements of a piece of music, or parts of a painting merged into the whole.

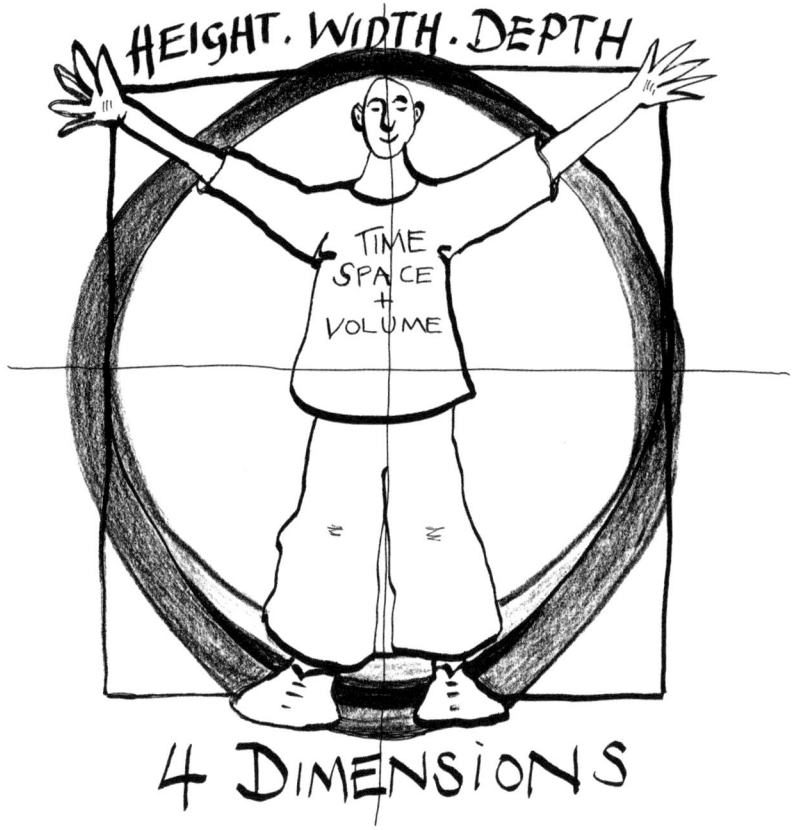

Our sense of volume: proprioception

In anatomy the three planes dividing the body are the transverse plane, passing horizontally through the body parallel to the ground; the median plane, dividing the body vertically down the centre into left and right sides; and the coronal plane, dividing the body vertically from front to back. Knowing about these three planes helps us experience ourselves in volume, in our height, width and depth. This is part of the often-unidentified sense of proprioception that we all have.

The sense of our body's movement is called kinaesthesia. Proprioception is our ability to sense space and location within us as well as our body's relationship to the space around us. It is important to balance the sense of our internal space, with the sense of the space around us.

A sense of volume within us can help us understand posture as an interrelationship of parts within the whole that will not be in a fixed position unless we become rigid or tense. If this happens, we can unfix and let ourselves return to a sense of easy volume with natural grace in stillness and movement. Once we begin to appreciate this sense of our volume, we can integrate this with the sense of the space around us. The awareness of space, within and without, helps develop an understanding of posture into an experience of poise.

Body mapping

We have a map of our body in our subconscious brain; we often mis-map where our joints are and this means our movement is less free and accurate, less efficient and can even cause injury. Muscles are there to create movement at joints. It's good to clarify where your joints are and the directions in which they articulate. We might be moving with an inaccurate body map, which makes us less well coordinated. We can re-map our movement and sense of being in space by consciously upgrading our body map. Having an accurate sense of where our major joints are means we can start moving in a comfortable and coordinated way. Embodying this information is fundamental if you happen to be human and live in your body. An example of this is finding where your head balances on top of your spine. To get a rough idea, put your index fingers behind your earlobes and tip your head backwards and forwards. This can give you a sense of where your head balances. Was it where you thought it was?

Grounding and releasing to our contact points

The way we bear weight in standing is fundamental and hugely influential on our structure and how we balance and move. We can feel a tremendous sense of safety from registering we are grounded. Grounding creates a foundation for being upright, symmetrical and available to reversibility when we move. This requires us to be able to bear weight as equally as possible over our two feet while standing.

Weight distribution and release into the contact points

1. Allow yourself to have a sense of contact with whatever it is that is supporting you: the chair through your sit bones in sitting; your feet on the floor in standing; your head, back, shoulders and feet when lying down. Let yourself have a sense of landing through your contact points whatever position you are in.

2. Avoid pushing down. Imagine a meeting between your contact points and the surface. It is good to find this sense of opposition, of support where we release through our contact points, but also receive the equal and opposite upward support from what is supporting us.

Confidence

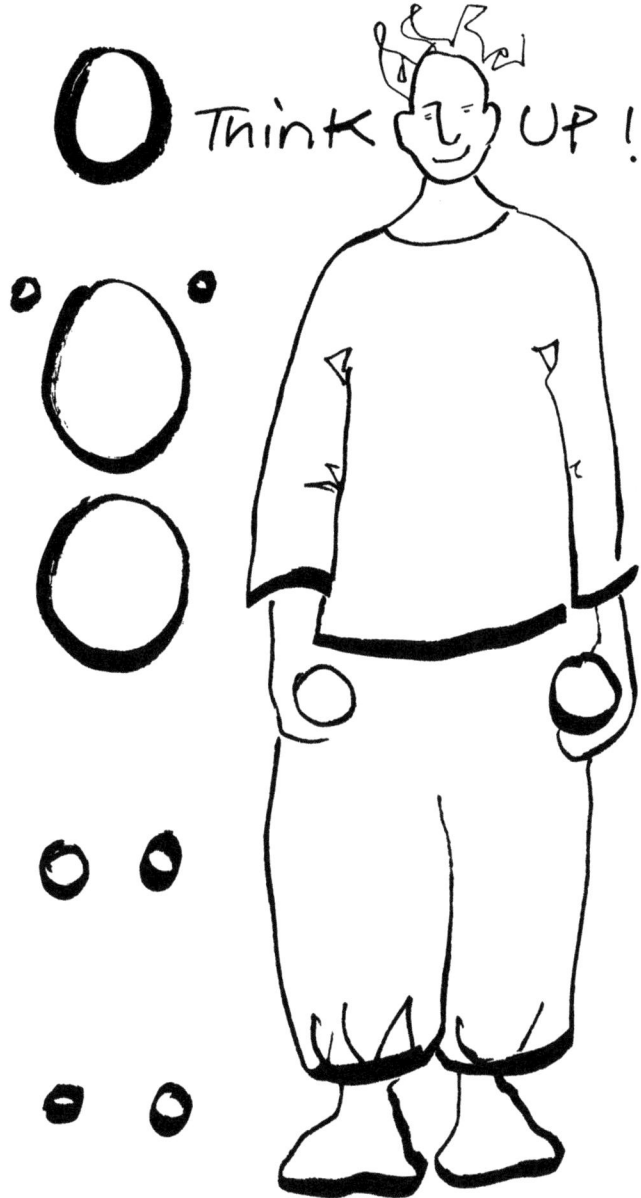

Many of us tend to stand on one leg and push out to the side with one hip, pulling down on the other side of the body. When sitting, we often pull down in the front of our torso or cross our legs and pull to one side. The trouble with these sets of movements or habits in the way we sit or stand is they become patterns that restrict joints and constrain movement right up through our body.

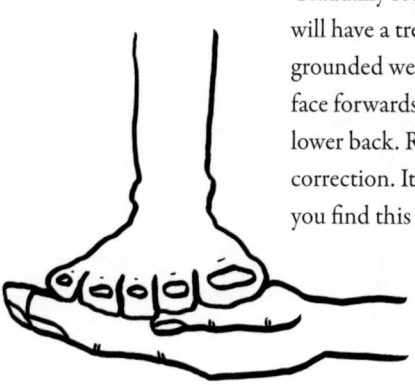

Gradually rediscovering grounding and balance when standing or sitting will have a tremendous impact on our everyday ease in walking. When grounded we can free our ankles ready to go into movement. Let your feet face forwards rather than pointing out or in, this has a big impact on your lower back. Remember to think in terms of creative connection rather than correction. It's easy to lose track of the sense of our hands and feet, and if you find this happens to you it is really good to rub or shake them gently.

Sensing symmetry while standing

1. Experiment with standing and balancing your head and spine between your two feet. Think of your whole footprint being on the floor, facing forwards, letting your spine rise gracefully upwards with your head balancing on top – like a tree with roots going down and the crown of the tree pointing upwards.

2. While standing the foot is like a tripod with the weight distributed over three points on the ground. These are the heel, the big toe joint at the ball of the foot and the ball of the little toe.

3. Connect to this sense of grounding and very gently take your weight over one foot and balance, then move to the other foot. See if you can sense the weight changing from the outside of one foot to the inside of the other, the gentle push away from one foot to the other.

4. Try leaning forwards and backwards over your ankles as though you are standing over a bridge. Let yourself be aware of your ankles being free and the weight changing in your feet as you move. This makes it clear that we balance over our ankles, not our heels, which are behind our ankles.

5. Finish by just registering your feet, releasing down, allowing this to create a sense of releasing up through your whole body.

Legs

Thinking about your legs can reveal various habits. To avoid locking them try to think your knees away from your lower back and hips.

The three levels of your pelvis

1. While sitting, try bringing your knees together (do you shorten your body?), then wide apart (do you push forwards in your torso?).

2. Notice how much your torso changes in relationship to your legs being in balance. Avoid crossing your legs all the time while sitting, even if this seems unnatural at first because it has become so normal.

3. If we cross our legs, we disturb the alignment of our pelvis. Find out where your hip joints are in relation to the top of your pelvis and your sit bones.

4. Put your hands on the crown of your pelvis and move your legs while you are sitting; notice your sit bones are still on the chair, so your hips joints are above them.

Soft and tall

1. Avoid locking your legs while standing – soften your knees, you don't need to bend them. Try thinking of letting your legs be in an easy balance.

2. Avoid standing only on your heels or toes, bring your weight over your ankles and let your heels drop down behind your easy ankles.

3. Think of standing over your whole footprint and having 50 per cent of your weight down through your heel, then 30 per cent on the ball of your foot and the remaining 20 per cent under the ball of the little toe.

4. Try just moving your weight from foot to foot, side to side; get to know the inside and outside edges of your feet.

5. Let this sense of grounding give you the feeling of springy legs, allowing you to be soft and tall throughout your body.

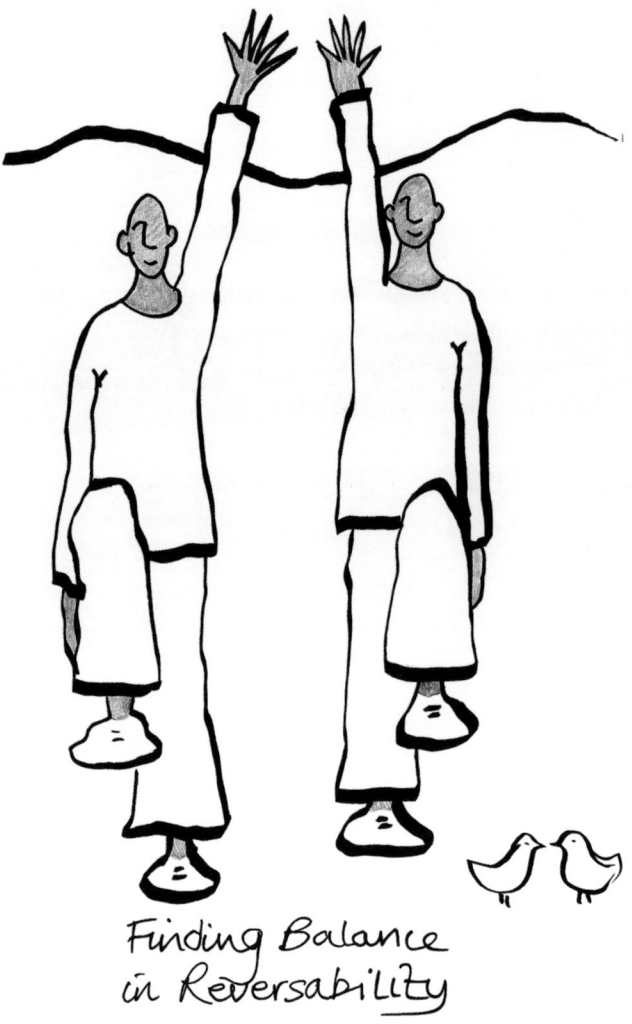

Finding Balance in Reversability

Experiment with having a standing desk. Many great creatives have done this: Ernest Hemingway often stood to write, Mozart stood to compose, Picasso stood to paint.

Standing in balance and ease is a skill for life.

Being in touch with your pelvis

Three main skeletal structures connect to our spine: our pelvis, our ribcage and our head. When standing our pelvis mediates between our spines and our legs, when sitting it is the contact point for our grounding. Being in touch with our pelvis provides a foundation for balance in both cases. It is really worth looking at some anatomy books and seeing the structure of all these different parts of you and where the moveable joints are. A useful book is *Anatomy in Action* by Theodore Dimon.

Confidence

Grounding while sitting

Remember, you don't sit on your legs (or your spine) in balanced sitting but on your sit bones, even on the sofa, when you can sit right back and be supported and easy.

Pop your hands under you to find your sitting bones and slightly pull the flesh out as you take your hands out from under you, to find yourself supported in sitting, by your sit bones.

Rocking

1. Again, find your sitting bones while sitting on the chair and rock from side to side, getting to know your sitting bones.

2. Think of your sitting bones as feet on the chair, take a few steps backwards and forwards on the chair with them to notice how this affects your pelvis, its two sides and your sacroiliac joints.

Finding your pelvis

1. In standing, try locking your knees and see the impact on your pelvis.

2. Try bending your knees to see if this pulls you down in the front of your torso.

3. Now allow yourself to find your grounding, your centre and think of having balanced knees – not locked or over bent, just easy. Let this support your spine to be soft and tall, allowing your pelvis to hang freely.

Centre

Centred implies being present and easy, calm and confident. Our centre of gravity is just below our tummy button, where our lower belly is. Our lower belly is in, and supported by, the bowl of our pelvis and our lower back. Rather like the black box in a plane, the lower belly can contain our emotional history; it reacts directly from the information coming from the emotional area of your brain telling you if something is safe or not. Recent research suggests that the opposite is also true, that signals from our organs – particularly our gut – play a major role in regulating our emotions. We can think of this as a sort of relay between our body and mind, both informing each other about our whole. We can restore ease by releasing our centre. For more information about balancing our gut and our gut reactions and the influence our diet has on us, read *Gut,* by Giulia Enders.

Releasing our centre

1. While sitting, release to the support of your sitting bones without losing your sense of being soft and tall.

2. Place your hand on your belly, letting this be free and available to breath movement, and tune into inner calm.

3. Try placing your hands on either side of the top of your pelvis – see if you can sense the bowl of your pelvis being supported by the chair, to allow your breath to move freely.

Confidence

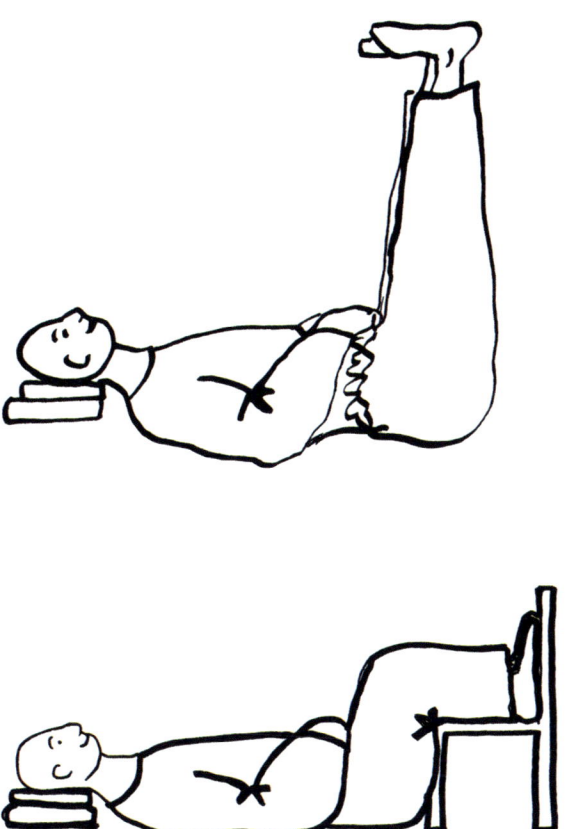

A great way to find your natural core and centre is using the floor for support to detect an ease in your lower back. This is an area in which people often get pain.

Finding strength in release

1. Lie on the floor in semi-supine (see page 40). Take time to rest in this and sense your whole back being supported.

2. Experiment with having your feet straight above you, which naturally engages core muscles.

3. You can also do this using the wall as support.

4. Another useful option is to support your lower legs by resting them on a chair while you lie in semi supine. This is great for finding a release in your lower back.

Avoid getting smaller

Are you always thinking you are too busy? Do these thoughts make you shorter, narrower, tighter or more held. Are we getting smaller and tighter? Again, this can often relate to feeling embarrassed, harassed, late and anxious. Take a moment to think about getting smaller. How does it feel? Is it an outdated strategy? Could it really be part of the bigger picture of a lack of confidence?

It's a big change from posture to poise when we think we are not trying to get bigger or taller than we are, but avoiding getting smaller – some of us are 6 foot 2 but walk around at 5 foot 10, but sometimes we are 4 foot 6 and try to lift up our ribcage to appear 5-foot 8... Let your spine have its height, be your width and your depth, head held high, taking up the room that you naturally take up. There are so many ways to try hard to get your posture right that aren't helpful, but once we are grounded, centred and have our primary freedom in balance we can just BE UP, quietly confident and easy. An ideal state is being present, noticing with a gentle curiosity what we are doing and how we are doing it. Connecting not correcting.

Sensing height

1. While sitting, place one hand on your head and the other under your tail bone. Move them away and notice how tall the space is between them. Is it longer or shorter than you thought?

2. Think of taking up your space while sitting or standing by being soft and tall.

Spine

Your spine is a flexible, strong, resilient structure. Our spine has volume and is full of articulating joints that stack into soft, lengthening curves that can bend and turn with ease. It is our suspension system.

The front half of the spine is weight bearing. We can think of this as our core.

Our spinal cord travels through the middle of our spine carrying messages from the brain to the body and the body to the brain.

Muscles attach to the front, back and sides of our spine making it very important for balancing and movement.

Confidence

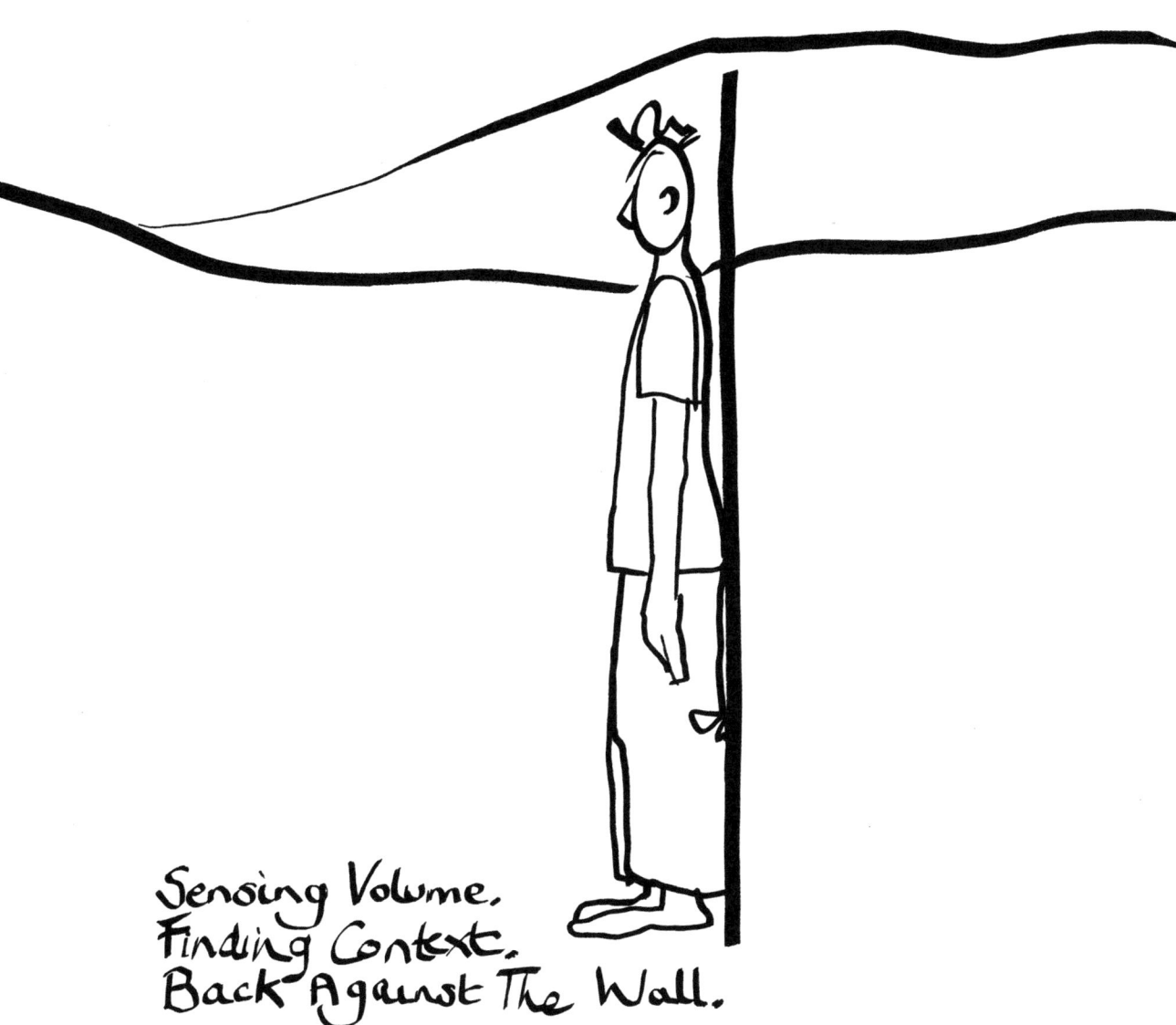

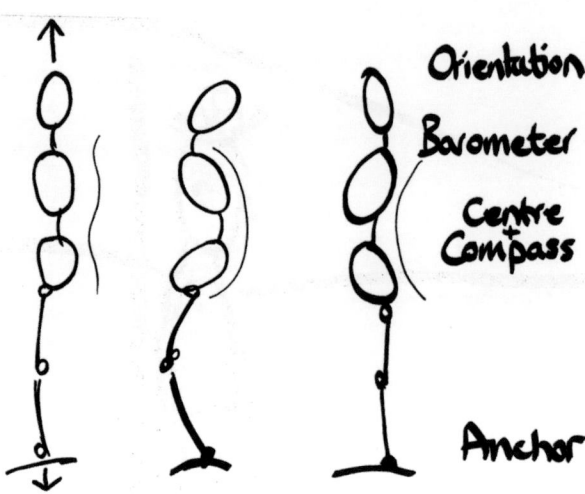

Bananas

We are the only animals on planet Earth with a lumbar curve designed to allow us to have suspension up on two legs. Acknowledging this curve without exaggerating it makes the suspension efficient.

1. Avoid pushing your lumbar spine forwards and creating a forwards banana.

2. Avoid pushing your lumbar spine backwards and creating a backwards banana.

3. The spine isn't straight; it has soft lengthening curves that create a spring and suspension in the body that means we can maintain buoyancy. If we overdo or underdo the curves of the spine we lose our height, width, poise and ease and the sense of spring that the spine's quiet strength gives us. When we are grounded, centred and have a primary freedom we can feel strong, light and confident.

If you're overwhelmed, upset, tired or bored, notice your resource to stop for a moment and close your eyes and breathe. If you have time, do your quiet mind, easy body study, or even better have a lie down in semi-supine (see page 40 and page 61) to restore your compass.

Click and direct

Sometimes associating a sound or action with a direction creates a new connection in our mind to a sense of our embodied compass.

1. While sitting, think gently of 'up' – try clicking your fingers and sending your hands up into the air to remind you where up is.

2. Send your sitting bones down, clicking your fingers down towards the chair.

3. Click your fingers away from your shoulders to remind them to widen.

4. Click your fingers away from each other forward and backwards to remind you to deepen and move. This helps us reconnect to a reliable sense of an embodied compass.

Our Back Stories

Your back story

Backs are particularly interesting, sometimes they push forward into the front space so it might seem like we have a large tummy or a pelvis that is forward of our heads. It is good to remember our backs also have a front, like the back wall of a wardrobe.

See if you can think of your back as inclusive of your spine, shoulders, ribcage and pelvis. Our bottoms in French are called derrieres and need to be behind us, not squeezed and tight and full of unnecessary tension. It is useful to think right down to the base of your bottom rather than just to your waist when you think of your back.

Thinking of your back being back tunes you into volume and strength. A tree does not collapse in on itself, and a good piece of furniture keeps its form and shape. This sounds a bit mad but very often our backs behave as though they are trying to be fronts. Let your idea of your back include your behind, so your back is like a large figure of eight. Finding this sense of your back staying back can be fun.

Confidence

Finding Resistance Hands on the Wall.

Back back

1. Think of your back going backwards, include the front of the back, this will include your lumbar spine and your pelvis.

2. Facing a wall, bring your hands up to shoulder height. Sense a little resistance forward as you press your hands to the wall. This gives you a sense of having something to release your back backwards from. This creates the easy sense of opposition of forces in the body.

3. With this gentle sense of resistance, think of taking your whole back back, then gently bring your arms down away from the wall as you rebalance to a sense of being back and up.

Thinking of walking backwards

1. Think of walking backwards and your back will go back.

2. Notice that just thinking this (and not actually walking backwards) has a big effect. You can even think this when sitting.

Sails

We can think of our backs as sails in the wind – flexible and curved, but not collapsing. While doing whatever you are doing, imagine your back is a sail that has caught the wind.

Torso and ribs

Give yourself a moment to notice how you balance in your upper torso, as this helps you see the quality with which your ribs are balanced and how much this area is responding to your emotions all the time. Thinking of your ribs and head being balanced over your pelvis can help you avoid shunting the upper torso out of alignment and symmetry with the lower torso. Your shoulder blades move gently around your ribs as you breathe. Remember, your heart is in your rib cage and you don't want your heart or ribs to become fixed.

Don't let your rib cage imprison you

1. Avoid lifting up your ribs in such a way that you stiffen or hold them.

2. Remember to let all of your ribs respond to movement of your breath.

3. Placing your hands on your ribs encourages them into movement and will help you notice how your ribs aren't all horizontal but some incline and hang downwards when you peacefully pause between breaths.

Ribs can be overlooked as a moveable structure if we think of them as a **rib cage**. It is good to remember they are constantly moving and are part of a dynamic relationship with our spines and fronts.

Directing your shoulders

1. Think about your shoulders – that can immediately put you in touch with them and you can then notice if you are holding or lifting them (nine times out of ten I am, and most people are, so you are in good company). Shoulders and necks are a classic place to store tension, so it's brilliant to develop this kind of awareness.

2. Now tune in and ask them to release and let go into their full width, away from each other, do not pull them backwards or forwards, up or down.

3. Let your head be easily and lightly balanced – you will notice that pulling your head down or up will interfere with your shoulders and neck being free. Noticing these interconnections helps us to think in terms of wholeness.

Finding Quiet Strength

Let your arms hang upwards

Arms

We can often forget to notice the quality of our arm movements. We might hold our lower arms up all day, tense up when we type, forget to let our arms swing when we walk. Sometimes we forget to lift our arms above shoulder level regularly and yet it is such a great stretch and a freeing movement. If we don't release regularly, we can get stiff and pulled down in our arms and torso, and this can lead to being uncomfortable and even eventually a frozen shoulder.

How we think about the structure of our arms can be revealing. Sometimes we might imagine our arms as separate from our shoulders, whereas they are deeply integrated like wings onto our torso. Our arm and shoulder structure is rather like a yoke balancing freely on top of our torso. Our shoulder blades integrate into our backs with muscles under them as well as over and, if we pay attention, they are gently responding to breathing, releasing rather like the opening and closing movement of curtains – moving out as we breathe in, in as we breathe out.

Arms also integrate with our neck and back via the big moving muscles at the front and back of our body. Our arms belong to our back as well as our front. When arms integrate into springy movement they are led by our free wrists and hands. Rather like those mittens we used to wear on a string going through our coat, our hands and arms are deeply integrated with our torso – we don't want to narrow our shoulders or upper arms but send our shoulders gently away from each other, away from the midline of our spine. It's good to lengthen and to widen.

A study of arm movement

1. Place your right hand on your left collar bone. Notice as soon as you lift your arm above shoulder level that your collar bone and shoulder blade move too.

2. Sitting in balance, have both arms by your sides. Now move your arms up and down, leading with your hands.

3. Try slumping back and down and move your arms up and down, and sense how heavy this feels.

4. Try arching your lower back and then lift your ribs, then lift your arms. Notice the extra effort needed.

5. Return to being grounded and centred again and notice how easy it is to lift your arms from here. Light, strong and free arms is what we are after.

6. It can be very helpful to have some soft balls (or socks) under your armpits to tune into the movement of breathing and let go of narrowing your shoulders.

The sphinx

This is a great way to release your arms and upper back.

1. Sit at your desk with some space on its surface where you can rest your lower arms, including your elbows.

2. Let your sit bones land on the chair, allow your spine to be soft and tall, see the room around you.

3. Let your arms feel supported by the table but not heavy. Imagine typing with this sense of ease in your structure, freedom in your hands, wrists and arms.

4. Let this go on to inform you to stay grounded and not pull your head forward, to the side or down when you use your arms.

Primary freedom

Our head weighs between 5 and 6 kilos and yet when we feel happy, purposeful or optimistic it appears to weigh nothing at all. Maybe we lose the sense of lightness and freedom of our head balancing on top of the spine (remember, your neck is part of your spine) because we relate so much to our mental chatter and zone out of being aware of the head as a part of our body in movement. We can push our neck forwards and pull our head back and down. We can slump and pull our head forward and look down. The good news is we can work with subtle directions to allow our neck to be free, which allows our head to release up into free active balance. Primary freedom of our neck and head, integrated with being grounded and centred, is key in the development of wholeness in our embodiment.

How we carry our head has a big impact on our alignment and coordination – think of the impact of the weight of our head down through the body. We might push our head forwards, hold it continuously on one side. Having our head freely balancing on top of the spine allows the spine to find its easy length and the back to find its easy width. This has a great impact on breath and movement. The head leads movement and the body follows. Having a free head, neck and back relationship allows our voice to become more resonant and reliable.

Confidence

Primary freedom equals a free relationship between our head and our body. Our head free to move in its orbit on top of our spine.

Think up

1. Experiment with thinking of your head releasing up into balance on top of your spine and release your jaw too.

2. The top of your spine is at about earlobe level and quite central. Just allowing your head to release up into lightness and balance takes a massive amount of pressure off your spine, your lower back and your entire nervous system.

3. Remind yourself where your head balances: put your fingertips just behind your earlobes and think of articulating the movement of your head from that height, the depth of the joint where the head balances being centrally located there.

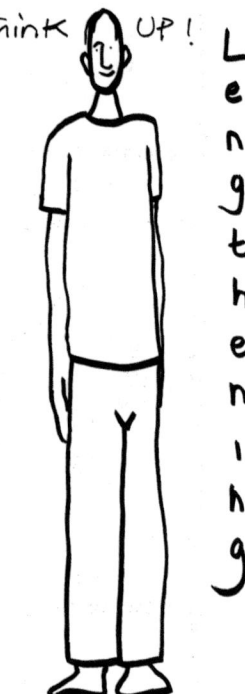

We see this beautiful free balance and integration of the head in relation to the body in children and animals. This supports the idea that we naturally know how to use our body as children and it is only later that we develop or learn less than ideal habits and become less coordinated and free. We are restoring our ease.

Thinking up is not an effort

1. In sitting or standing, try pushing up – feel the effort and push, then let that go. Notice what happens to your head and neck if you do this.

2. Now try pulling down, then pushing up. Notice how your head will be involved in these movements.

3. Experiment with just thinking up and easy, soft and tall. If you are very slumped you will be able to gently release up to your natural height with your head leading your torso. If you are over-lifted, you might need to re-anchor to your sit bones to let go of holding up or pushing forward in your body. Notice the quiet strength, dignity and ease of being in balance.

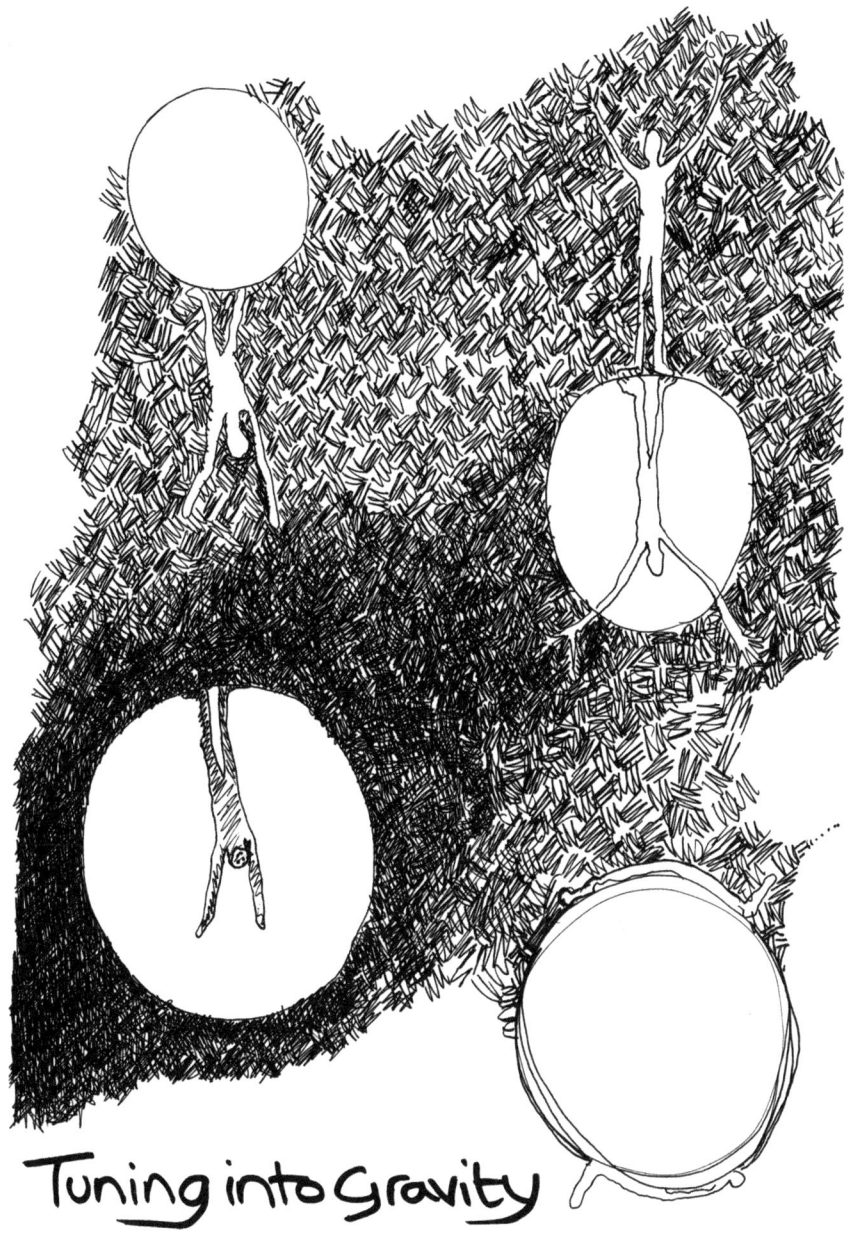

Gravity

Gravity is the force we move in; it means that like a tree we grow upwards and yet are rooted into the ground for support. Tuning into both forces of gravity and levity allows us to feel grounded and confident, released from feeling we must support ourselves, but that our structure is designed beautifully to balance us in conversation with the force of gravity. Let yourself tune into that force without pushing or pulling, let your feet be down and your head be up at the same time. After all, many natural structures don't struggle to be easy with the force of gravity, so be inspired by animals, trees and plants.

Spacial Awareness
Anchor, Compass, Orientation

Spatial awareness

The temptation is to correct, but let connection and curiosity be the order of the day. To notice ourselves and how we are and what we are up to is a much more sustainable approach. There is a lot of movement in stillness and finding that still point in the turning world also means noticing we are always breathing – and if we don't get smaller or fix, we can let all the other movements inside us be free to move. Muscles have this tremendous capacity to fix and tighten; letting them be in just the right state of ease is brilliant, rather like the fullness of a peaceful, still, summer evening. Think of your grounding rather like your anchor. Your easy upright spine is like having your compass in tune and your awareness of your space and the space around you rather like your orientation to your volume and the world around you.

Anchor, compass and orientation

1. Stop, think, connect, see, breathe and balance, notice your grounding, centre and primary freedom, then let yourself be aware of the space above you.

2. Notice the space behind you.

3. Notice the space to your sides.

4. Notice the space below you.

5. Enjoy the sense of space you take up as well as your awareness of the space around you and beyond. This helps us stay connected to being present to ourselves and the big picture of the world.

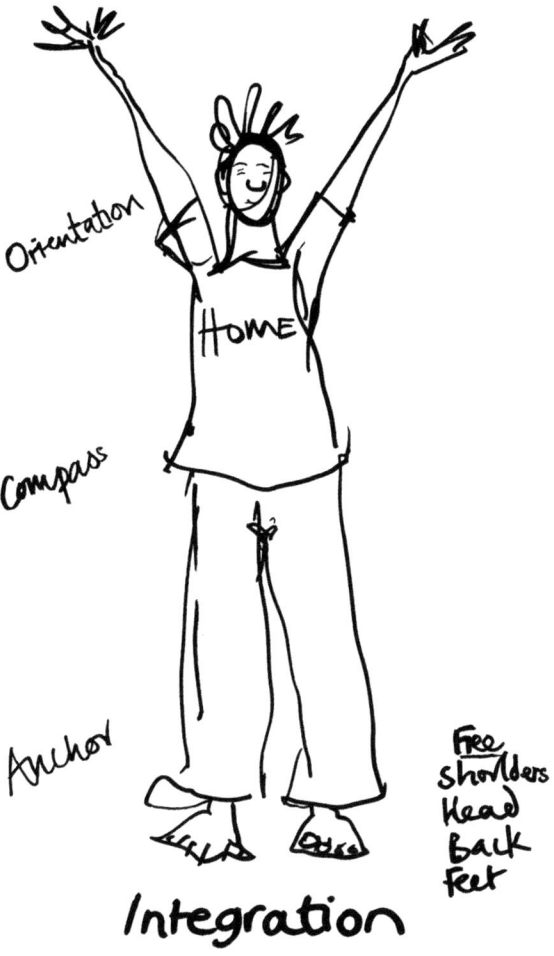

Being, breath and emotion

Life can't always be perfect. There are many ups and downs, griefs and anxieties. Stuff happens. The idea that we should be happy all the time can lead us to feel disappointed, or as though our emotions are wrong. Being comfortable with the reality that we will all probably feel uncomfortable some of the time and learning to be at peace with this can be so helpful. It can help us identify how we feel and why, to determine what we need and what the next choice could be. We might just need to rest, digest and process what has happened and know that things will change again. We can let ease arise from finding this quiet strength.

Breathing has a big effect on our general health, our energy, skin and digestion. For thousands of years humans have been regulating their health and emotions through their breath. When we feel our emotions change, our breathing changes, just as altering our breathing changes our emotions. When we can, smiling has been proven to help us breathe more freely.

Thankfully and wonderfully, breathing is a reflex, so we don't have to remember to breathe. However, sometimes we can get into a habit of only breathing in a particular way and holding on to our breath, so it's useful to remember that we can change these patterns back to ease. It's very important to respect breathing, because although we are the only animals on the planet that can consciously affect our own breath, it takes time to negotiate this if you are not used to doing it. Overthinking breathing can make us anxious or uncomfortable, so take it slowly. Sometimes you might enjoy closing your eyes to be more in touch with your breath, but only do this if you can also stay present in the moment and in your body. This helps us to feel safe.

When our beathing is shallow, holding our abdominal muscles and stomachs in and restricting our ribs, we can become extremely anxious. However, we don't want to over-breathe, as this can make us feel lightheaded and even faint. A useful thought is: if in doubt, breathe out. Lengthening the out breath slows our heartbeat and usually helps us to become calmer.

Thinking of your breathing as movement might be a big change, so experiment with thinking less about getting air in and out and more about interacting with your inner movement and integrating this with your outer structure. Let this movement be slow and low in your torso, as this helps self-regulation – especially if you feel upset about something. Finding your slow-released breathing movement, expanding and releasing in your lower belly, your back, your solar plexus, your rib cage and the whole of your torso – your armpits, too! – all this even in our smaller breaths can be life-changing. Remember, you don't have to do this all the time, just get to know your breathing patterns gently and slowly over time and trust this will return you to ease when you might feel under threat or pressure.

Every breath is different, and a wonderful website for a deeper unpacking of breathing can be found at www.artofbreathing.eu. Another great source of information about breathing is the book *Breath*, by James Nestor.

Breath: how it works

An easy awareness of your breathing means tuning into the conversation that goes on between our inner movement and our outer structure. Knowing how this works can make all the difference. Our **in** breaths slightly speeds up our heart and our energy, and our **out** breaths tend to slow our heartbeat.

The main muscle of breathing with a central area of tendon is the diaphragm. Knowing clearly where it lies and what it joins to and how it moves can be useful. Our diaphragm forms a dome-like shape just underneath the lungs and the outside edge of our diaphragm connects to our lower ribs. Along with the heart, the lungs take up most of the top of our torso. The top of our lungs are just above our top rib and they extend lower in the back of the ribcage than the front.

It is great to experience how our ribs rise and release differently on every breath, and that we don't need to lift them. See if you can include thinking about your floating ribs – which are your lowest ribs, quite low in your back – when you breathe. Being available to movement will make breathing easier if you don't try to lift up the ribs.

Diaphragm: finding our inner tempo

The diaphragm flattens downwards as we breathe in and domes back upwards as we breathe out. Think of your ribs like bucket handles moving up and out on the in breath and releasing back to rest with the out breath.

1. Make a dome by interlocking your fingers to reflect your diaphragm, at about solar plexus level, and imagine your forearms represent your ribs.

2. On an inhalation, flatten your hands and let your elbows spread outwards to exemplify the journey of the diaphragm; on the exhalation, release the hands up and let the elbows return your hands to the dome-like shape.

3. Do this a few times and let your arms and your breath slow down by lengthening the out breath. Notice how you can slow your inner tempo by slowing the movement you are making for the out breath. Peacefully pause between the out breath and the in breath.

Finding Quiet Strength

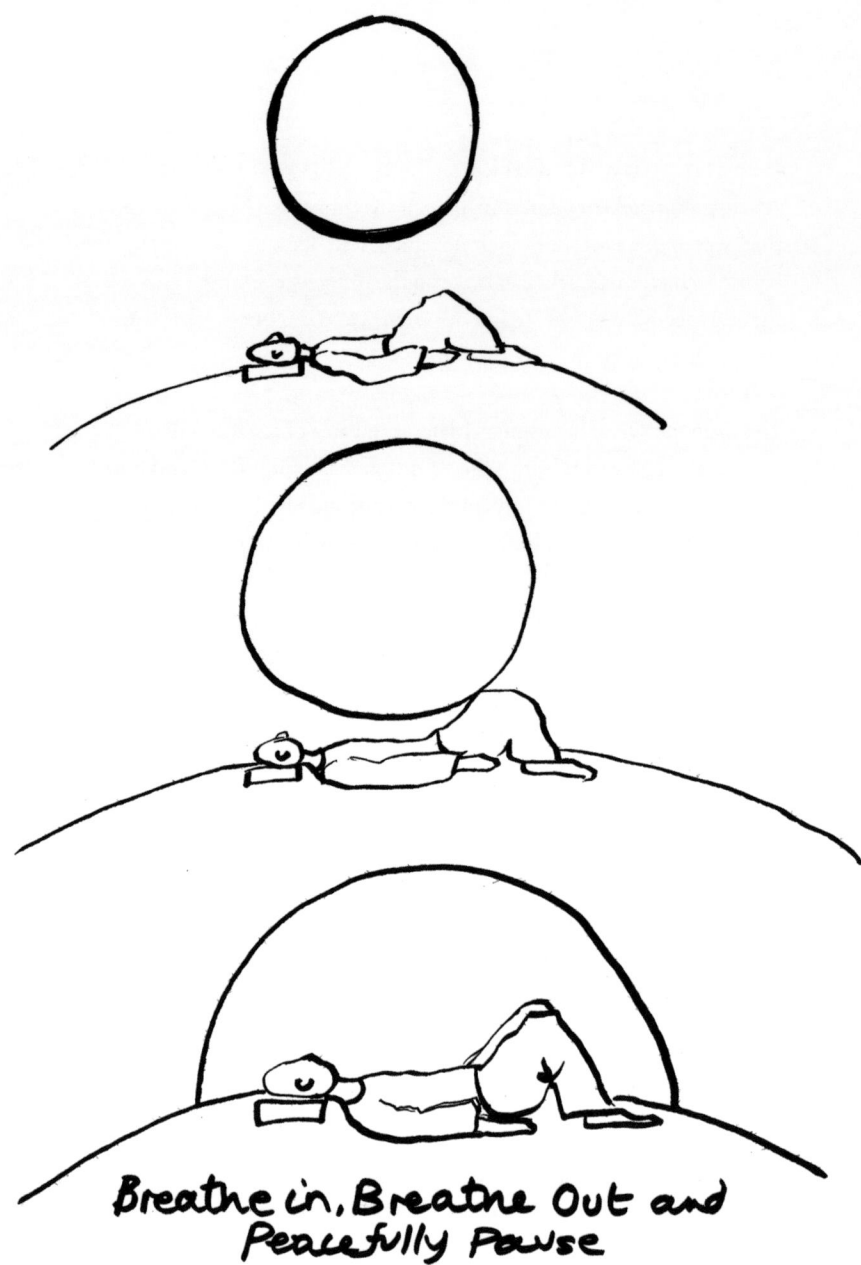

Breathe in, Breathe Out and Peacefully Pause

Breathing is movement
The breath is a natural reflex. Our nervous system organises our reflex breathing movement. Out of our neck come the all-important phrenic nerves which travel through our torso to the diaphragm; another important and compelling reason to allow our necks to be free, as this freedom is so influential on our breathing.

When we release, we can let our breathing happen to us. All our ribs join into our spines at the back, creating a widening expansive movement when we allow ourselves to breathe. We often only think of breathing in the front of the body, but our lungs are three-dimensional and the breathing movement happens in all directions. A lot of our breathing movement is also in our armpits and sides of the body.

Tuning in to the movement of breathing

1. When you lie down, sit or stand, see if you can tune into your back widening and releasing back as you breathe in.

2. It's reassuring to place your hands on your belly and on your solar plexus to sense this connection to breathing and movement in the front of your body. You can also try putting your hands on your forehead and heart.

3. Place your hands under your armpits then around your shoulders and just enjoy listening to the movement expanding outwards to the side.

4. Come back to quietly integrating a sense of the breath expanding you gently in all directions and allowing you to be soft and tall as you breathe out.

We might have the habit of breathing through our mouths. Nose breathing is usually the most positive way to breathe. Unless we are exercising, singing or playing a wind instrument breathing through the mouth normally means we over breathe. Breathing through the nose slows our breathing and heart rate down, keeping us calmer and more regulated.

Mouth breathing is common in asthma sufferers. It's useful to know about the Buteyko method. This is a method to re-educate your breathing. It uses various techniques to encourage us to reinforce the habit of breathing through the nose. For everyone, just registering nose breathing and integrating with the body's movement of breathing is so positive.

Remember, you don't need to pull your torso down to breathe out, or lift up to breathe in, stay soft and tall and let the breathing movement happen. No need to consciously sniff or gulp air. Breathing in semi-supine is a great, safe way to explore breathing (see page 40).

Being present with our breathing

It's easy to overthink breathing and get into a panic. Remind yourself that breathing is a reflex action and if you sit calmly or lie down, breathing will happen. It can have the sense of waves coming in and out, each one a little different, but pleasurable. Remind yourself that the peaceful pause comes after the out breath. It is good to remember to smile as breathing becomes easier, because in so doing we slightly flare the nostrils to receive breath.

Nose breathing

1. Close one nostril with your finger and breathe in with the other nostril, then swap your finger to breathe out on the other side.

2. Do this a few times, swapping around.

3. Notice how this clears your nose and helps calm your breath.

The wave

1. Breathe in and out through your nose if possible. Let the wave of movement begin low and release up through your body. As you breathe in, your diaphragm goes down as your body releases and opens outwards.

2. This becomes a lovely opposition, a natural force of equilibrium. Let this easy breathing and tuning in to the natural forces happen while you are lying down, so that you can feel supported, and perhaps listen to some music and let this restore you to ease.

3. Try this with your eyes closed if you can stay present.

Easy breathing

This is another way to slow down the out breath and coordinate breath and movement. Imagine the easy structure of your breathing and upper body moving freely. Slowing down the out breath tunes us into our parasympathetic nervous system (see page 24) and calms us down, so that we can feel grounded, centred and present, so it is great to do before a meeting or a performance, or just while the kettle is boiling, or you are listening to the radio.

1. Stand with your feet about hip width apart. Connect to your feet on the ground. Start by putting your hands under your armpits and sense the movement of your ribs as you breathe.

2. Take your hands down and as you breathe in lift your arms up your sides to over your head and breathe out slowly through your mouth as you take your arms back down. Peacefully pause, then breathe in through your nose, taking your arms up again.

3. Do this a few times, really enjoying breathing in and slowing down your out breath. Let your arm movement connect to the tempo of your breath. This can recharge and reset you back to feeling calm and confident.

4. You can do this in sitting as well as in standing.

Big Breathing

Regulating the breath

Being able to slow down your breath or find energy through the breath is a bit like being able to put the brakes on or press down on the accelerator. The main thing to avoid is pressing both pedals at the same time.

The sigh of relief and connecting to the peaceful pause

Letting yourself regulate through slow, longer out breaths should be a birthright.

1. Let yourself sigh, it's such a nice thing to do, and notice if when you sigh your body pulls down. See if you can stay soft and tall while you breathe out.

2. See if you can sigh and then have a peaceful pause, before you breathe in again through your nose.

3. Try blowing out softly and easily, smile, then breathe in through your nose.

4. Try making the sound 'Ah' while smiling and breathing out, allowing a twinkle in your eye as you smile. Repeat and enjoy.

5. Also try humming on your out breath while smiling if possible or try singing and enjoying making sound, this can be so enjoyable.

6. Thinking of taking the time to consciously speak on your out breath is a great way to put natural pauses in our conversations and slow down to enjoy speaking and listening. Often, we don't take a break when we are chatting and we can get breathless and even forget to give the other person space to talk.

Revving up energy

The great news is that breathing, as well as calming us down, can also gently rev up our energy if we feel tired or bored. We might be bored because we are not breathing freely. It is always good to be thoughtful about breathing. It's good to start with lying down while working with breath energy.

1. In semi supine try breathing out on an VVV, FFF or an SSS sound, moderately vigorously. Close your mouth at the end of making the sound and peacefully pause. Sense the gentle engagement of the out breath in your abdominal muscles while you do so, then release your abdominal muscles and centre with the impulse of the next beautiful in breath.

2. On a short rhythmic pulse, breathe out four short ss sounds and then one long breath counting to four: ss ss ss ss sssssssssss. After this out breath, peacefully pause before allowing the breath in. Notice letting the in breath come in through your nose. These breaths can help us notice our resilience and how to stay strong and easy.

3. Remember to laugh – it's one of the best breathing releases ever.

Gratitude

Lots of ancient wisdoms use breathing in to think of receiving what you need and breathing out for letting go of what you don't need. Breathing in thoughts of gratitude can be a lovely practice and something that's easy to forget in this trammelled world. Feel gratitude for loved ones, for nature, for happy times, for when the washing machine works. This exercise can include really directing your chosen thoughts and not letting your mind wander off to anxiety or pressure. If those types of thoughts turn up, breathe them out. At first this might sound a bit 1960s, but it really helps and can restore feelings of belonging and being valued, reminding us that we are capable, valuable, loveable, powerful and equal. Remember, the more you grow a way of thinking, the more skilful it will be for you.

If we are feeling ok, it is sometimes important to just remind ourselves that we are ok. It is so easy to forget and feel we must walk on our knees across deserts for a hundred years and that we are not worthy. Tuning into breathing can help us make positive choices.

Finding Quiet Strength

Breathing as meditation

It's great to think of breathing in energy and breathing out anything you don't need. This can help us restore our self-value and self-belief. You can practise your quiet mind, easy body routine lying down and then release into a more lengthened quiet meditation (see page 115). Meditation can be done while sitting or standing and usually works with the breath in stillness. Meditation can be done in movement, too, for instance in walking meditations, which can be calming and restoring.

Coordinated movement

The embodied sense of movement and ease

Coordinated movement

The embodied sense of movement and ease

The importance of movement cannot be overestimated; movement can be medicine, it can help us embody change and create energy. It is wonderful to have movement practices, such as tai chi, yoga or a sport, as well as think about our everyday movement and how it integrates with our breathing. There is growing evidence that movement helps with our mental health, too. Muscles move us, breathe us and tell us how we feel. It's great to be structurally balanced so we can restore ease to our muscles and enjoy coordinating freely and moving easily.

Apparently, it took us five million years to stand up on our own two feet. Understanding the various elements of movement can help us to see the different forces at play. Movement is one of the ways we can regulate ourselves – our lives can crowd in on us, our thoughts accelerate, at which point it's time to stop, think, connect and choose. Most of us sit for too long each day, and just getting up and walking around can help take the pressure off our body and mind.

Movement can take so many forms and everybody will enjoy different ways of expressing movement. Some people love running and sport, some of us love slow, flowing movement. It can be so helpful to have a repertoire of movement to practise and enjoy.

Observe movement compassionately

It is sometimes hard to judge whether our coordination is going well. If we are involved in something that absorbs us, we can lose touch with our coordination and be unaware of the component parts of the activity that we are involved in. The important thing is to find our sense of quiet strength, ease and coordination so that we can feel connected, grounded, light and free.

Let yourself compassionately arrive at a non-judgemental way of being with yourself and observing yourself in movement, it can really transform your progress with your coordination. Try looking in mirrors not to notice how beautiful you are (which you are, by the way) but to also be aware of

Coordinated movement

whether your head is on one side, or if you are balanced over your two feet. See if you can just observe this with interest and absorb the information rather than immediately trying hard to correct. This may go along with a pattern throughout your body, for example being pulled down on one side, a habit that we can change.

What we want to do is acquire the information in a way that encourages us to accept ourselves and enables us to go on to develop our poise. Of course, it can be very useful to explore coordination with a movement teacher and take on board their supportive feedback when that is possible. It is vital to develop a positive, helpful model of feedback for ourselves for this to be a useful and sustainable experience. Remember to acknowledge progress. Notice every time something feels and seems a little easier. Once you can trust yourself to be onside with yourself it is easier to unpack what we do and how we do it. I recommend keeping a twinkle in your eye for observation. Remember that this is what talented people practise – non-judgemental observation that can lead to great personal development and self-belief. You can practise seeing what changes when you think differently.

Finding elements of movement

Understanding how our body moves helps us to develop an easier relationship with movement. We could think of these elements of movement as embodied aspects of the laws of motion.

Paradox

When two things that seem like polar opposites are true at the same time and just need balancing it can be a liberating thought after momentary confusion. It is brilliant to know that we have a body that has real structural strength at the same time as an easy flow and elasticity. As with the mountain and the river, the oak tree and the reed, two types of strength inhabit our bodies: lightness and freedom alongside grounding and connection. Allow your strength to include fluidity; allow up to include down, notice that you can think one thing and add another thought and live with them both harmoniously. Within our body we can enjoy these paradoxes as benevolent oppositions.

Opposition in direction

Opposition is a dynamic force in the body that really strengthens the harmony of our structure in stillness and movement. For example, notice that we can think down and up at the same time. If you think down through your feet to the floor let yourself be soft and tall through your body, right up to your head. There are lots of ways to direct oppositions in our embodiment, and these help us find a beneficial resistance and elasticity through our body.

Opposition to create volume and movement

1. Stop, think and connect to your balance in standing, think your feet down and your head up.

2. Think your whole back, back, going away from the front of your body. Imagining the volume in your torso.

3. Think of your shoulders widening away from each other and the central line of your spine.

4. Think your knees away from your hips and your back, not locking or tightening them.

5. Now release into walking and flow, enjoying seeing, breathing and balancing.

Turning

Opposition doesn't have to happen in a straight line. We can learn from the spiral arrangement of the muscles around our skeletal structure to find symmetry and reversibility in dynamic and flowing movement. When we are symmetrical and balanced, turning movements become easy and reversible, and we can have a sense of spiralling upwards as we turn to the side.

Rediscover this feeling by standing in balance and turning slowly and gently around your spine from side to side, letting your arms be free to swing, staying up and easy as you turn.

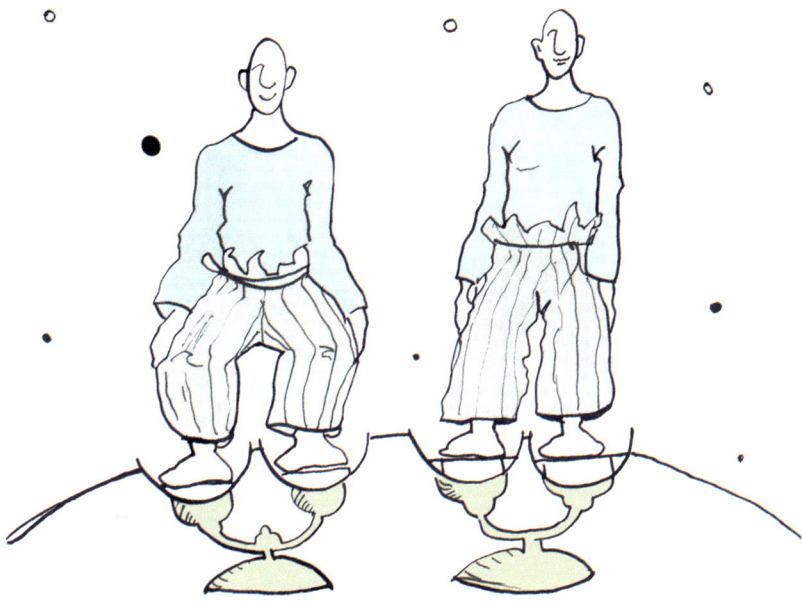

Rebalancing

Working in balance is a useful idea as it's easy to lose confidence when we lose a sense of balance. Avoid staring or over focusing your eyes when you are trying to find balance, or tensing in your mouth or neck. Keep in touch with the ground while rebalancing.

1. Notice moving from side to side, left to right, on your feet and how the weight transfers from one foot to the other. Allow a little release down in one foot to move you to the other foot.

2. Notice the outside and inside, the perimeters of both feet on the ground. Let this become gently active as you transfer weight in movement. This is very good practice for letting grounding be alive. Come back to balanced easy stillness noticing both feet.

3. Now have one foot forwards and one foot back, knees springy, and let this little lunge allow you to transfer weight backwards and forwards – again, notice there is usually a little extra connection and release down in the foot we move away from, as we move to the other foot.

4. Experiment with stepping forwards and backwards with one leg, keeping the other foot supported and on the ground. Notice how this helps you experiment with being grounded while maintaining your balance in safe movement. Swap sides, noticing the difference on each side.

Finding Quiet Strength

Reversable
Releasing into Movement

Leverage and momentum

The leverage at your moveable joints gives a wonderful sense of articulation, rather like opening a paint tin with a screwdriver. When we have the right leverage at our joints it can help us find the right momentum and speed for the activity and movement we are in. Notice you can slow down and speed up movement but that will need a slightly different sense of momentum. Being grounded with your back back (as discussed on page 67) helps, whatever speed you are in. Much articulation while walking happens at our ankles.

1. If they are stiff or your calf muscles are tight, a good little tip is to stand on the bottom stair, or on the edge of a book, on just the front of your feet and let your heels drop down. Notice how this allows your lower back to release and lengthen. Your whole spine be soft and tall. The back of your legs to lengthen.

2. Then on flat ground try walking on the spot by bending each knee, lifting just your heel from the floor. This can be a great way to sense your ankle movement. These joints help us transfer weight and release into locomotion; they transfer weight through the footprint as we walk.

3. When you come to stand, think of sending your heels down. Allow yourself to feel length in your spine and fullness in your back. We want to balance over our ankles, not over our heels, to be ready to release into walking.

Connecting to five everyday movements

Knowing how to bend easily in everyday movement when our habit might be to bend at our waists not at our hips is invaluable and brings an intelligence to everyday life. This requires us to allow our legs to understand us and let ourselves recognise when we lock our legs. When you release your hips, knees and ankles, it's much easier to keep your spine upright and easy. There is a Chinese saying that all our happiness resides in having strong springy legs! Notice how much we can use springy legs and a soft and tall spine during the day. It's great to feel fitter in everyday activities and makes them more enjoyable, too.

Springy legs

1. Try this by a wall: have your feet an inch away from the wall and lean your back gently onto it, let your spine stay soft and tall and bend your knees up and down as you slide up and down the wall. Notice when your legs lock how your spine changes and you can go into a forwards banana. Notice which bit of your back is on the wall – ideally it should be your lower back and pelvis plus the upper back, and there will usually be a little space at your lumbar curve.

2. With your springy legs bent while your back is on the wall, lean your whole spine forwards, lead with your head, and release your hip joints, avoid pulling down in the front of your torso. Come back to upright using the release in your feet to find leverage and momentum.

3. Try this away from the wall. This is a great way to re-imagine how we could move well to make beds or clean the loo. If it feels easy, gradually release into a squat – this is great for picking things up off the floor (gravity is always working). Being able to bend with free hips and a strong back feels good.

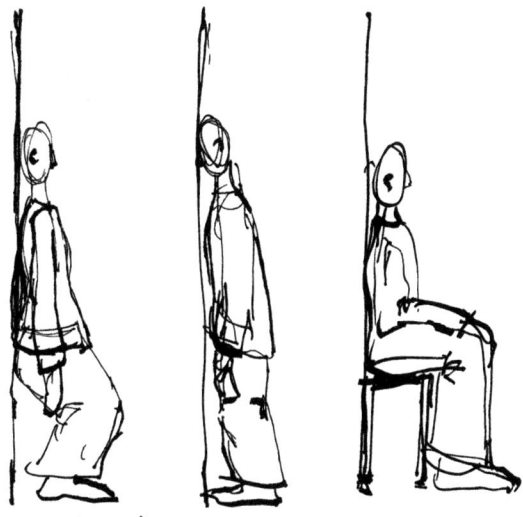

Wall work, finding strong, springy legs.

Finding Quiet Strength

The Lunge
Rebalancing by finding your height width + depth in stillness + movement

Lunge

We tend to associate this everyday movement with fencing, but it's actually a movement we often see well-coordinated people use. The push and pull gives a satisfying sense of movement and it can unlock the forces of ease and energy (and is useful when cleaning the floor, too).

1. Put one foot into the crook of the other and take a moment to balance, then release weight into the back foot, lift the front foot and step diagonally forward.

2. Notice you are in a beautiful balance between the two legs, as if your legs are springs.

3. Enjoy moving your weight back and forth in your feet, keeping your legs springy.

Coordinated movement

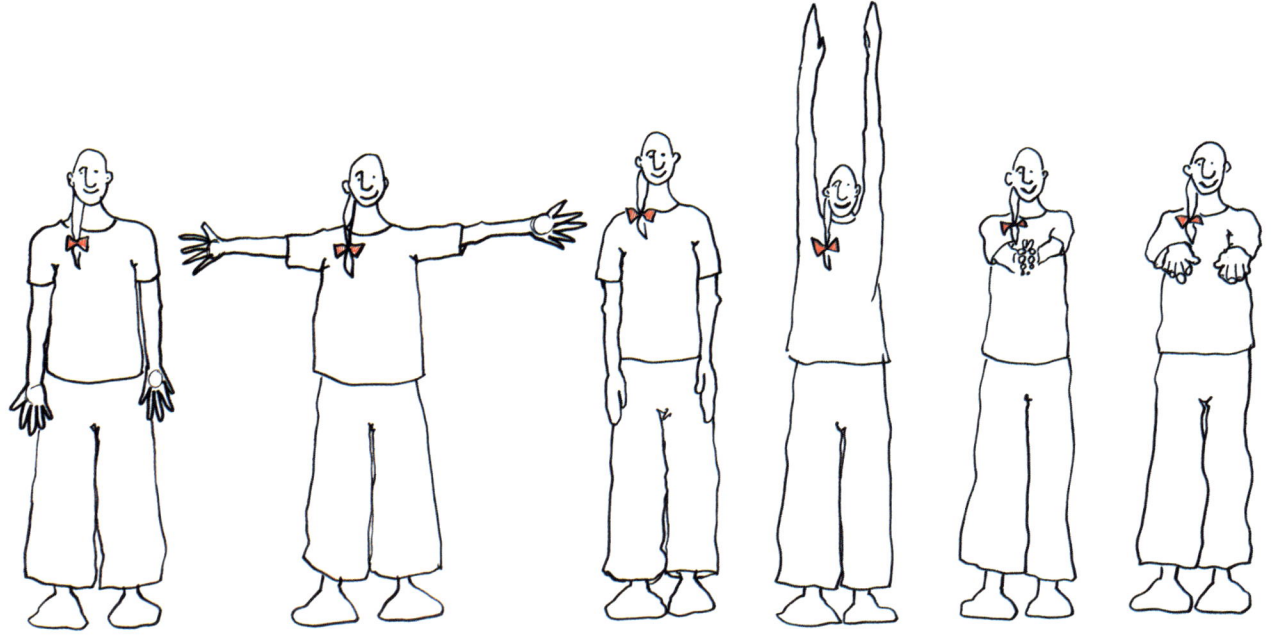

Easy arms above your head

Leading with your hands, take your arms above your head and gently look up, then stretch up through each arm towards the sky a few times on each side. Bringing your arms down on your out breath, look out to the horizon, leaving your head balanced and easy.

This movement experiment might help you notice how you lift your arms and whether you pull down when raising your phone to your ear or when you are typing. It's good to stay up and easy by stretching up through our arms, as we often need to stretch up to cupboards or to change light bulbs.

Getting in and out of a chair with poise

This is a great daily activity to be aware of, as it helps us notice how we transition from one state to the other. We can practise this movement to find efficient articulation and grace.

1. Stop, think and connect, see, breathe and balance before getting in or out of the chair.

2. Experiment with not using your arms to get you out of a chair but really let your feet and legs take the work of release and support in movement. If you are sitting easily, your spine soft and tall, you can let your head lead your spine to come to standing.

3. Once your head is over your feet, staying back in your back, let your heels release down during this movement. We are using the forces of leverage, momentum and velocity in this movement. Being aware means we can come gracefully to standing, a movement we do many times a day.

4. Try the same while going into sitting down. Stop, think and connect, to avoid pulling down in your front or shortening your neck and lifting your shoulders, and let your legs do the work. Stay soft and tall in your torso as you release and bend your legs into sitting.

5. The chair can also be a good prop for finding resistance and ways to connect to finding strength and ease, by having your hands resting lightly on the back of the chair and thinking your back, back.

Finding Quiet Strength

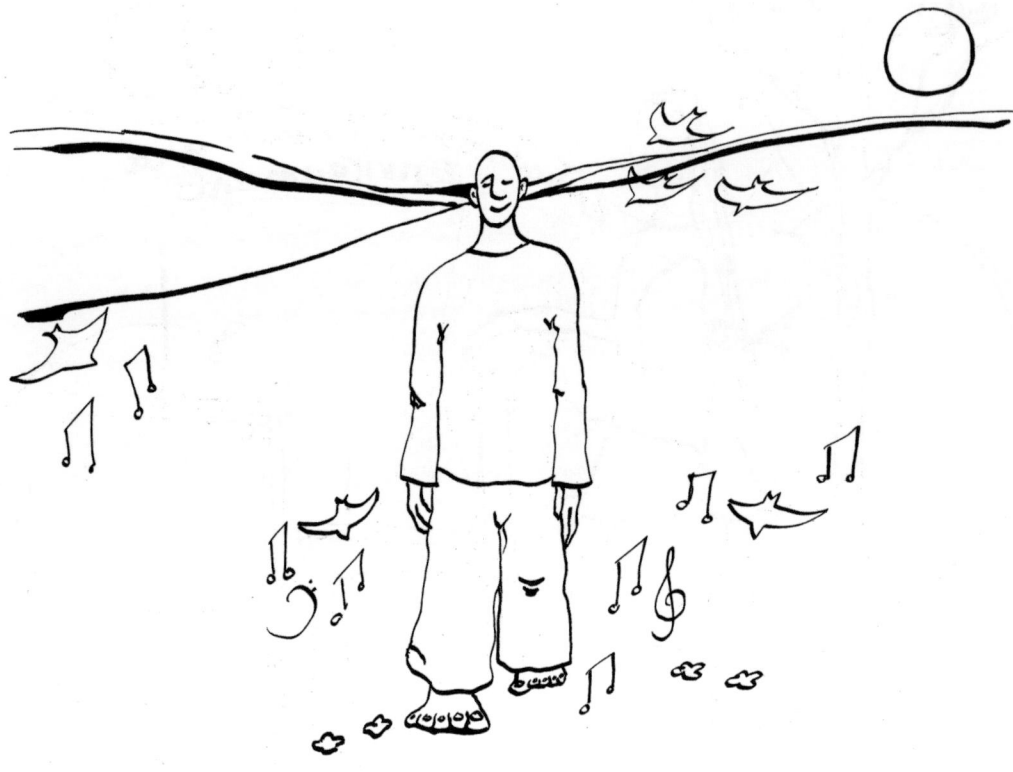

The joy of walking

Walking is a wonderful activity for coming back to ease in our mind and body. Part of our heritage of being upright is this free rotational movement. How we walk depends on how we stand, so tune into the rotation around your spine, try to let it be even, as this allows it to be reversible in a balanced way, not pulling down in the front into a backwards banana, nor lifting your rib cage up into a forwards banana.

1. Walk contralaterally – with your opposite arms to legs swinging. You can practise this in walking on the spot (not travelling with your feet).

2. When you walk, look out, see the world around you. Notice how this helps you move more freely.

3. Face your feet forwards, pointing in the direction you are walking. Observe how the direction of your feet affects your lower back. Notice how when we walk freely, there's a lovely sense of cogging through movement, a bit like a well-oiled clock.

4. Avoid over-thinking. Enjoy the movement, letting it all happen freely.

Coordinated movement

Walking with awareness

1. Try going for a walk with just your phone and keys and avoid always walking with a bag pulling you down on one side so you can find an easy symmetrical swinging movement, with your free arms and legs swinging in a rhythmic harmony with each other.

2. Practising walking backwards is a useful skill, as you only need to take one or two steps backwards to get a strong sense of your back releasing back, not pushing forwards. See if you can transfer this sense of your back staying back as you walk forwards.

3. See if you can stay in touch with nose breathing while you walk, release your belly and your ribs as you move and breathe.

Movement practices

Some of this book is focused on becoming aware of everyday movement and the choices that are always available to us. It is also hugely beneficial to our daily lives to have a movement practice that we can focus on that is separate from the rest of our lives. This can be a sport, martial art or a practice like yoga or Pilates.

Having a gentle movement practice that can be done even while waiting for the kettle to boil is great for helping us to remember the value of staying connected to movement.

There is much more understanding of wellbeing in sport these days. The 'no pain, no gain' attitude is thankfully not quite so common among professionals with their array of coaches. Those of us wanting to be involved with sport and letting it enhance our lives in a more recreational way, can find it as useful as professionals do to think about form. Form includes mental health, being calm and confident, as well as fitness and physical health and being well-coordinated.

It is wonderful to be inspired by the great ease of iconic sports people. The best competitors usually have a grace about them and are more interested in their whole self coming into play. Often the long game includes the inner game of sportsmanship; sports psychologists can help people with their mental attitude towards their game, and the impact of this on their physical form can be dramatic.

The power of changing our perception and motivation on our coordination is quite remarkable and can of course be applied to any activity. Rather like Zen in the art of archery or in the art of flower arranging, we come to understand what being in the zone really means. A sense of quiet energy, purpose and peace, a flow in an activity, where we are motivated by the sense of being in the present, rather than just under pressure to win.

An interesting book that talks about form in running is Malcolm Balk's *The Art of Running: Raising your performance with the Alexander Technique*, alongside his book, *Master the Art of Working Out*.

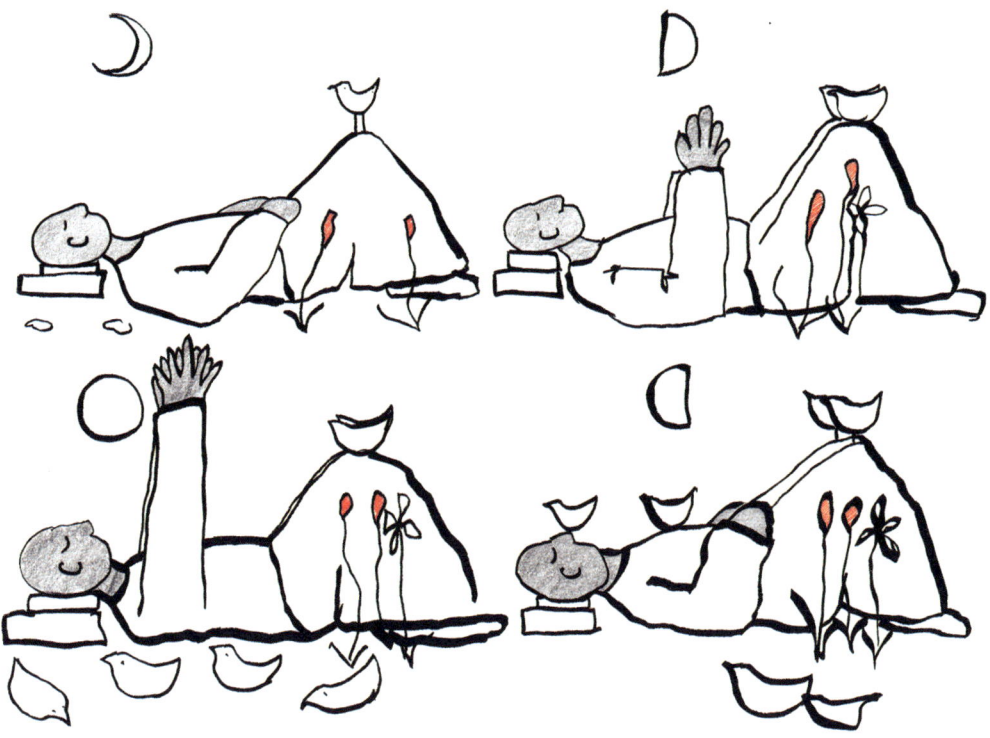

Dart

Dart work is a safe, gentle but powerful way to work on your movement and coordination. Professor Dart was an anthropologist and archaeologist who discovered one of the early hominid skulls in South Africa. Through looking at the body as a whole, he was also one of the first people to describe the double helix structure of the musculoskeletal system in the human body. He had some Alexander lessons that he found inspirational and went on to further unpack developmental movement. He created a series of procedures that help to re-establish an understanding in our body of how to coordinate well, going on to collaborate with Alexander teachers Joan and Alex Murray, to further develop them. These procedures work by moving through the developmental childhood reflexes that we all move through as we mature into upright walking, but sometimes part of the development can get left out. The procedures actively help us notice being very right- or left-sided in how we move, whether we pull down or lift up, and how we can turn and move symmetrically. Again, it's good to stop, think and connect and watch your inner tempo through the movements.

Here are a few to start with. Remember, it's as important to think through coming in and out of the procedure as the procedure itself. If, when coming out of any of these activities, you feel dizzy, put a hand firmly on the top of your head. Notice how this helps you settle and to feel grounded again.

Semi-supine

1. Without rushing, think through releasing your weight as you come to lying down with your back on the floor, a book under your head, knees bent and feet on the floor.

Semi-supine plus

1. Lie in semi-supine, releasing your back back.

2. Leading with your hands upwards, keep your elbows on the floor, stay like this for a moment or two, and let your shoulders release.

3. Take your hands up towards the ceiling, let your shoulders lift off the floor, then release them back down to get the sense of how broad and easy your shoulders can be.

4. Return your elbows to the floor and again release your shoulders, then bring your hands to your abdominal muscles and release your shoulders.

5. Slowly turn your eyes to the side and let your head follow, then, take your arm out to the side. Then reverse this on the other side. This is good for finding symmetry in the way you move your head and arms.

Full supine

1. Take your time to get down on to the floor through kneeling and rolling onto your side, then roll onto your back with your legs on the floor. Notice the effect on your lower back when you lie fully stretched out like this, then change to semi-supine with a book under your head. Notice how this integrates your whole back to the floor like a large figure of eight.

2. Let yourself rest here and get the sense of your back releasing towards the floor as it responds to gravity and to your breathing. Notice the front of your body being free and open and available to breathing movement. Sense your head being supported and how your neck can be free and tension free.

Rolling

1. Take a moment to lie down on your back.

2. Choose which side to roll onto, leading with your eyes and head as you take your arm out on the floor to the side that you roll towards. This can be very freeing for your shoulders as your release them.

3. Roll onto your side with one arm outstretched and the opposite leg bent up at 90 degrees towards your chest.

4. Find your contact points to push off and lean back to roll over onto the other side. This type of lying on your side is ideal for sleeping. You can try this with the arm out above your head for an extra sense of extension.

Child's pose with head movement

1. Kneel on the floor then sit on your bottom on your heels, with your forehead as near to the floor as possible.

2. Let your arms stretch out forwards and sense your breathing movement. Make sure the back of your neck is long and let your eyes look backwards towards your tail.

3. Let your eyes move from side to side slowly to feel a beautiful release in your neck as you allow your head to follow your eye movement.

4. Rest in the pose, finding quiet, then bring your arms to your sides. This gives you a great sense of grounding and safety.

Finding Quiet Strength

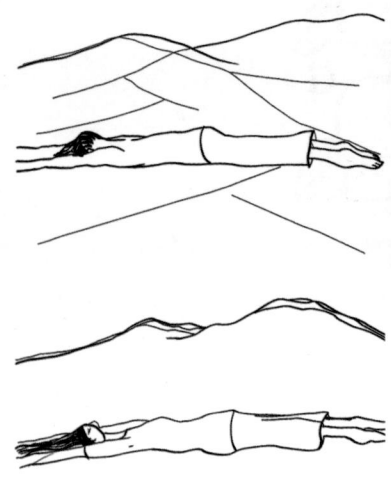

Prone

Lying prone (on your front) is how some people sleep, and this is fine if you can turn your head easily both ways. Much of our lungs are located in the back of our body and it is important to allow freedom of breath movement in our backs to be expressed. You might need a little support under your forehead or chest if you are not used to this position. Have your arms down by your sides.

1 Take a moment to let yourself release on the floor face-down. Let your arms be by your sides with the palms facing upwards and notice the openness in your chest and shoulders, the resistance the floor gives you to sense your breathing movement in the front of your body. Notice how we could consider this while upright.

2 Take your time to roll to the side slowly and come to upright with grace, noticing the moments when you will need to release weight into your arms, legs and feet.

Finding the Range of Movement, when our head leads and our body follows.

Rolling over in a chair

1 Sit in a chair, legs hip width apart, and really connect to your sit bones – try putting your hands on the top of your pelvis to sense this (see page 57).

2 Take a moment, look down, letting your eyes lead your head till you are hanging over your legs. Only go as far as feels easy. Sense the length and ease of your spine. Let yourself notice your belly releasing forwards into your legs, your back widen as you breathe.

3 When ready, look at your tail and keep looking down as you roll gently back and up to sitting, as though slowly stacking your vertebrae up. Don't rush.

Coordinated movement

Tai chi

Be as the still mountain; move like the great river. Lao Tzu

Tai chi is an ancient martial art, a practical philosophy in movement that reflects how to negotiate the stimulus of life. It gives you a regular sequence of movements, which you can trust will tune you into being present and help you find grounding and ease.

A sequence of movements creating a form is usually practised solo or in pairs, at first very slowly, but the tempos can change and reflect the idea of maintaining a sense of awareness at any speed. The big principle of the form is to work with internal energy, which the movements of the form are designed to gather, store, deliver and balance. This energy is understood as the forces of yin and yang. These can relate to so many aspects of life and nature – push and pull, masculine and feminine, dark and light – the harmony comes through finding the balance of these opposing forces.

The practice works with the fight stimulus and response, mirroring life's challenges and interactions. My tai chi teacher, the inspiring and wonderful Michael Spink, said that what this martial art teaches you is how to avoid conflict and find harmony in life. It is the most peaceful of practices. The art of tai chi works with free-flowing movement from a very strong sense of grounding. The principles are so useful to apply to our everyday lives and can really change not just your sense of grounding, but also your balance, ease and awareness. I would highly recommend finding a local group and teacher to practise with regularly and a little time and a quiet place to practise at home.

Like many ancient wisdoms, tai chi finds quiet strength in movement and stillness. Tai chi emphasises moving with the breath, which tunes us into moving with an awareness of breathing integrated into movement. This discipline is linked to Taoism, a philosophy with its roots in China, based on an understanding of the natural world and its forces that impact upon us. Tai chi has a poetry of movement that can be beautiful to watch.

There are many beautiful principles in the philosophy associated with tai chi, of freeing and breathing, alignment and connection, being present with your attention, sensing and listening, and an emphasis on being and not over controlling. In movement the principles of tai chi embody our sense of grounding, centring and primary freedom, as well as interconnecting soft strength and freedom.

Tai chi classes often include working with chi kung, which literally translates as 'energy work'. Chi kung is a practice that coordinates breath and meditation through movement.

Here are a few movements drawn from chi kung and tai chi that you can try.

Staying in touch with your dan tien

Dan tien roughly means, centre of energy. There are three of these, one in the head, one in the chest and one in the lower torso. This lower torso energy centre is the focus of this exercise.

To stay in touch with your lower dan tien is to stay in touch with your centre of gravity, three fingertips below your tummy button and three fingers in. For a moment, sit or stand with your hands just below your tummy button and imagine tuning into that centre. Let yourself notice how your dan tien integrates with breathing, expanding and releasing like the sea.

Find centre + Feet on the ground + Head in the air

Open tai chi – Sung

Sung is the name of a stance where we lower our centre of gravity and keep our legs springy and grounded.

1. Stand and let yourself be grounded, let your legs be springy (not locked or straight, not over bent). Have your arms by your sides, then breathe in as though up through your feet.

2. With your in breath, let your arms slowly rise up and out in front of you to chest level. Bring them back towards you and then down slowly on your out breath, releasing your breath as though through your body and feet. See if you can keep in mind the ease and release of your dan tien.

3. Let yourself gently see out into the distance with your eyes looking slightly low towards the horizon. Do this ten times and then take time to absorb the quiet connection to your whole self and the world around you.

The Gates

This idea tunes us into our volume and the sense of space around us.

1. Stand quietly, connected to the ground and your lower dan tien, imagine you are standing as if there is a gate in front of you, not too close so you can still sense the space around you.

2. Take a moment to breathe and then imagine there being a gate behind you. Breathe again and notice the gate to the right and left of you.

3. Take more time and space to breathe to orientate yourself to this sense of a compass the gates can give you.

4. Now imagine the gates diagonally to the front left and right and then the back left and right. Stand for a while and let yourself absorb the sense of space this gives you.

Three swings

There is a video of these on my website, they are brilliant for releasing your spine and exercising equally the muscles of your back. Start by standing in balance, weight equal.

1. With your feet facing forwards, hip-width apart, let yourself turn and swing around your spine, slightly transferring your weight from side to side. Let your arms release and your hands gently thwack your back as you turn from side to side. Do about ten swings on each side.

2. Pause. Now turn from side to side as before, this time rotate your foot out and in, with your heel on the ground, toes in the air, and the weight will be over the supporting leg that doesn't turn.

3. Pause. Now turn by bringing your heel into the centre and out again by turning on the ball of one foot at a time. Imagine keeping the rotation close to your spine. Experiment with different tempos.

Waving hands through clouds

1. Stand, feet wide apart and with an awareness of your grounding and sung.

2. Bring your arms up in front of you, let one hand be above the other – as though you are holding a large ball, palms facing towards you.

3. Now turn your body to the right, letting your arms lead the movement to the sides. Once you are over towards one side, bring the upper hand down and the lower hand up and turn and reverse the movement other way. Like fluidly waving hands through clouds. There is a video of this movement on my website.

4. Go slowly and imagine you are threading moments of awareness through the movement rather like rhythmically threading a string of beads.

This classic movement can be done very slowly with an integration of the breath, the tempo can be taken up then down again. Notice how turning freely to both sides is like a beautiful metaphor for having an open mind. Changing tempo reminds us to find equanimity at any speed.

walking slowly, being present, helps us notice releasing + rebalancing

Mindful walking

1. Find a space where you can take a few steps.

2. Take a moment to become aware of your grounding, dan tien and the sense of a golden thread gently connecting to your head, rather in the way that a puppet string allows the puppet to suspend down from support while also staying up and easy.

3. Taking it slowly, from standing, let one foot come forwards to the ground and touch the ground but not put weight on it, as though you could lift the foot up again if the ice was too thin. Let yourself really register the weight staying grounded on your back supporting foot.

4. When you are ready, let the foot release its weight into the floor and transfer the weight towards this foot, then gently step through with your back foot. Taking a few steps forwards in this way, now try this slowly going backwards.

There are many interesting variations on mindful walking, which help us think of balance in this actively measured way. Doing this exercise we can find a presence with being grounded in movement. This gives us a sense of peace in movement. This feeling of grounding is thought-provoking; do we really hold our ground in a peaceful way? Are we always too busy to breathe and connect? Experiment with this slow walking while having your hands on your back or tummy for a deeper sense of the movement of gentle breathing. This is very helpful when working on finding balance.

Connecting to heaven and Earth

1. Interlace your fingers down in front of you with your palms up, breathe in and lift your hands to lower dan tien level (around the bottom of your solar plexus) on your in breath, then turn your hands over and breathe out as you press them gently downwards, connecting to the sense of the Earth and ground.

2. Your fingers still interlaced, take your hands out and up in front of you with your in breath, to over your head, feeling a gentle stretch to an idea of heaven and the sky above you, then unlock your fingers, letting your hands lead in a big circle to your sides as they slowly return to your sides on the out breath.

3. Let this movement and breath connect you to a sense of strength, integration and spatial awareness.

Yoga breath, body and picture

The word yoga means to yoke together, and this ancient wisdom yokes together the connection of breath and movement. It is a wonderful practice and can build long-lasting strength and ease. The great news is you don't have to do it for hours a day to feel the benefit. As with many of these ideas of building a sense of our embodiment, a little done regularly makes more impact than hours practised occasionally. I am introducing a few poses here that show some of the range of the practice. It's important to apply your means to yoga, not overdoing it, staying present and connected. Let it be a restorative practice rather than a competitive sport.

I find with my students that balancing the strength poses of yoga with ease builds a repertoire of different energies that we need. Go gently if you haven't done any yoga before. It is always best to practise in person with a group because the energy is supportive. Find a non-slip mat or floor to practise on so you can feel very confident you will be able to stand without slipping, and wear easy, comfortable clothes rather than anything restrictive.

Yoga practices can vary and there are so many out there now, free and available on the internet. My practice is in the Iyengar tradition and includes standing poses, floor work and meditation. Here are a few poses that can be practised for 10 to 20 minutes a day. Usually the practice of the poses regulates a very important understanding, that backbends tend to rev up our energy and forward bends usually help us to calm down.

Yoga also introduces us to learning how to stretch and not overstretch, to balance the forces and pulls available throughout the body. Again, avoid lifting or pushing your body, be interested in volume and expanding forces in your body. Let the breath connect to the energy of gentle stretch and movement. Balance the poses on both sides to create a symmetry of connection. Be as interested in getting in and out of the poses – that is still part of the practice – and remember to tune into time, space and ease. Stay present by seeing, breathing and balancing so you can sense the right amount of time in the pose for you. With practise, this will gradually extend.

There are many beautiful writings on yoga and many local classes. It is useful to balance the practice to what you need. Use it to develop your skill to stop, think and connect to your quiet mind and easy body, to finding your grounding centre and primary freedom before you start each pose and see if you can weave this awareness of wholeness into the poses. Most sessions usually end with some time in meditation to bridge the energy between your practice and the everyday. End your yoga practice with a moment of quiet, if possible, in lying down or sitting.

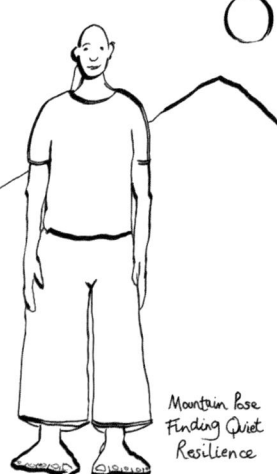

Mountain Pose
Finding Quiet
Resilience

Mountain pose

1. Stand with your feet together facing forwards, distribute weight over the whole foot, have your arms by your sides and just be there, grounded and aware of your space and the space around you.

2. For a few moments, find a slight sense of stretch throughout. This is the basic standing yoga pose.

3. Now release and gently stretch your arms above your head for a few moments and return your arms to your sides. There is so much to enjoy in this simple pose, consciously standing and being present, aware of the weight and lightness. It helps us to inhabit everyday standing with dignity and strength, inspired by nature.

Finding Quiet Strength

Triangle

1. Stand with your feet hip width apart, on your out breath take your arms up to shoulder height, palms down.

2. Step your feet apart and turn your right foot in a 90-degree angle to the right side and turn the left foot slightly to the right.

3. On your exhale, bend your trunk over to the right side, bringing your right hand towards your right knee or ankle if you can, your left arm above your head. See if you can let your legs stay strong and your torso lengthen on both sides.

4. Look out to the front and if you can look up to your left hand, stay there for a few moments. Release down through your feet to come back up to standing. Then repeat on the other side.

This pose is good for strengthening legs and finding an upwards release along your spine and torso even when you are not upright. These poses gives us energy when we might be flagging.

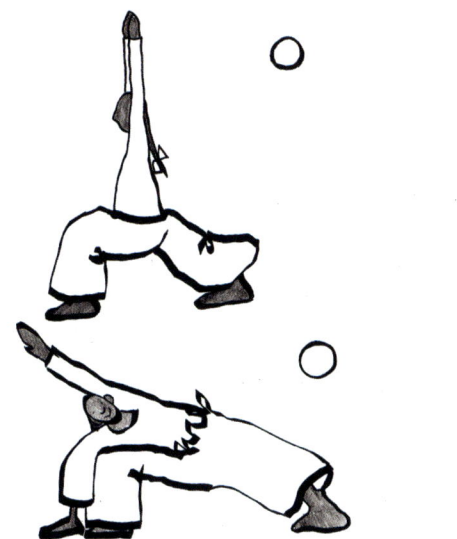

Tree pose

Balance poses are great: many of us need to work on our everyday balance.

1. Stand in your basic pose, then mindfully take the weight to your right foot, grounding with great awareness.

2. Lift your left foot up to your right knee – or above the knee if you can. You can either bring your hands together in a prayer-like way then stay and balance there, or take your arms above your head to get an extra depth to the balance. This pose tones your leg muscles and gives you a sense of balance and poise, rather like the dignity and wisdom of a tree that doesn't have to try hard to stand up.

Star pose arms up

1. Stand with your feet as wide apart as possible.

2. On an in breath, take your arms up above and slightly in front of your shoulders. Think of extending out to your hands, through your legs to your feet and up through your spine and head.

3. Turn your palms to face the ceiling, then after a moment face them forwards and after a few breaths back to facing the floor, then bring them down to your sides. Enjoy the sense of movement in your shoulders and releasing out through your hands, feet and head.

4. Take a moment to come back to standing. This pose is brilliant for finding volume.

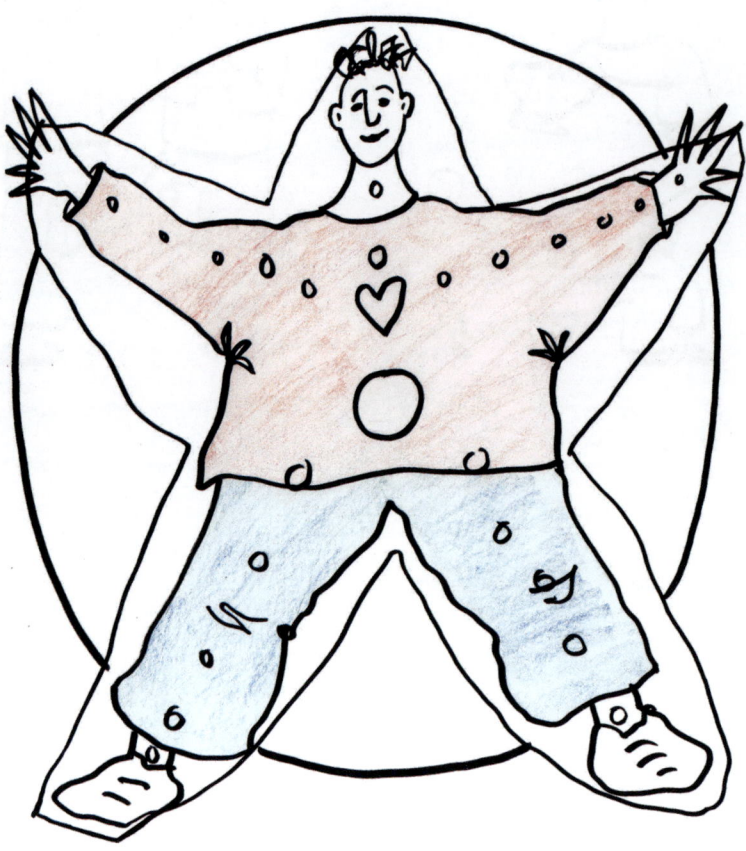

Starfish

1. Have your feet hip width apart, then rise up onto your toes, keeping a sense of the ball of your foot. Take your arms up as you breathe out, then back down as you breathe out, bringing the whole of both feet to the floor.

2. This time, think of being a starfish as you go up onto your toes, think of opening equally on both sides of your body, and again breathe out as you come down. This helps with keeping a sense of flexibility in your ankles and a connection to the ball of your foot while finding balance as you stretch up.

3. A variation is to go up on your toes and stay on your toes as you bend your knees, then bring your heels down, then feel the release down through your feet as you come up to standing.

Coordinated movement

Backbends

1. On your mat or a carpet, lie face down. For a moment let yourself experience this release. Always go slowly and gently with backbends.

2. Bring your hands up to shoulder level on the mat and lead with your eyes, gently look up and out forwards, let yourself come up a little on your arms, keeping your elbows on the floor.

3. Let yourself assertively look out, then turn your head from side to side a couple of times and gently look down, bring your head down and come to quiet. This opens our chest and shoulders and gives us a gentle backbend which usually gives us a little more energy. It is also good to sense the independence of your head and neck relationship, rather like a four-footed animal. Backbends also show us, when we go a little beyond our range, how we might be slightly pushing our backs forwards all the time. This, alongside forward bends, helps us restore a sense of upright ease in everyday life and helps to balance our energy.

Forward bends

Forward bends are very good for restoring calm and finding flexibility in your spine.

1   Stand with your feet hip width apart, your legs slightly flexed and head looking down.

2   Let your head be led by your eyes, roll and release down into a forward bend.

3   Stay hanging for a while, release your arms to let yourself find a free release in your head, neck, shoulders and upper spine. You can fold your arms to get a little extra weight into the stretch.

4   Keep looking down as you roll up, really letting your head be the last thing that comes to upright, looking out in front of you. If you feel at all dizzy (very common), place a firm hand on the top of your head. You can also do this sitting in a chair. You don't have to get very far forwards, that's not the goal, the sense of release is. This helps calm us down.

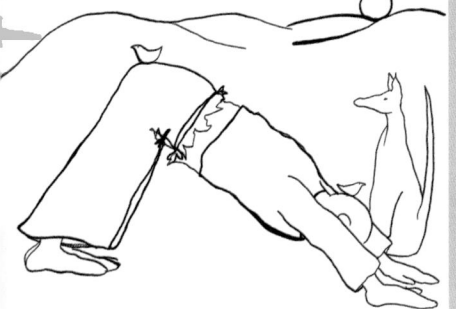

Dog pose

1   Start on the floor on your hands and knees. This is known as table pose and it is a great way to strengthen and lengthen your spine horizontally.

2   Now tuck your toes under and release down through your contact points, to bring your weight back towards your feet, with extended arms and a little weight through your hands. This gives you a beautiful extension and direction through your spine and arms in one direction and your legs and feet in the other direction.

3   Take your time in this quiet, powerful pose to extend and lengthen your spine, releasing further into the pose with the breath.

Coordinated movement

Lying down

Most yoga sessions end with a period of lying down, to allow you to quietly absorb the energy of the session and return to your day. It's good to do this because you can strengthen your back and restore your quiet strength naturally by resting.

Finding Quiet Strength

Understanding the Embodiment of Wisdom and Emotion.

Curiosity

Integrating our senses

Curiosity

Integrating our senses: being present in the wider field of attention and awareness

Sensory appreciation is not always as celebrated as intellectual achievement and academic success, yet we all get so much enjoyment and purpose from our senses through art, music, food, fragrance, colour and touch. Letting these elements of sensory awareness be valued in our lives can be a wonderfully peaceful and fulfilling way to return to being present. It is good to remember that we receive information through our senses. If we let the information come to us, tuning into our senses rather than trying hard to perceive the information, we can become more aware of ourselves and our surroundings.

About half of our nervous system is sensory. Sensory awareness has usually only been thought of as including the five senses but as we have been discovering, we also have our senses of movement and spatial awareness as well as our all-important sense of humour.

Sometimes our senses can become a little faulty or dulled. We might have blind spots and we have probably all had the experience of seeing a snake and finding it is a stick; this can extend to all our senses, and we may just not be aware in a reliable way of how we are receiving or including them.

The American thinker Frank Pierce Jones described being present with our minds and the senses, including our body sense, as being present in 'the wider field of attention and awareness'. This wider field means we can pay attention to an activity we are doing, like cooking or writing an email, but have a lively sense of our embodiment as well as of the world around us at the same time. In activity we can be aware of our feet on the ground, our breathing, a sense of living in time and space. It really is gold dust, as then we can notice our poise, our effort and adjust and recalibrate to ease.

Socrates referred to this integration as 'the common sense' – being present with all our senses acknowledged. It is so easy to lose touch with sensing and get caught up only in analytical thinking or past and future thinking as our preoccupation. We have many senses that can be included in bringing us to being present, the sense of space in our bodies, everything contained

within our skin and, of course, the acknowledgement of our smell, touch, taste, hearing and vision.

Cranial nerves

Our brain and spinal cord make up our central nervous system. We then have our peripheral nervous system that extends out of the spinal cord into our torso and limbs. Our peripheral nervous system includes twelve pairs of cranial nerves that connect key functions directly to the brain and do not travel via the spinal cord. These twelve pairs of nerves connect with the nose, eyes, ears, tongue, face, neck, plus the all-important vagus nerve. What does this information mean for us? It is like knowing about the superhighways of connection. Our cranial nerves are key in relaying sensory messages back to our brain, where it is processed, as well as organising motor action in response to this information. It is so positive to let ourselves come into harmony with these messages from the senses.

Smell and memory

It can be calming and uplifting to have nice smells around. Today there are lots of candles and house fragrances available that are not chemical and really do have an effect on our mood. We only have to register a tricky smell to notice how much it can affect our body; we often cringe at the very thought of it. Smell also has a powerful link with our memory; choosing to have a fragrance that reminds us of lovely moments is such a constructive thing. If you sit at your desk, it is sometimes good to squirt a nice fragrance into the room to change the energy. Best of all, though, is going out into nature and sensing the wonderful aroma of plants, rain, grass and trees.

Taste

See if you can savour the sense of taste. Taste covers so many aspects of life, but we often forget to find the time to really absorb and delight in it. There is a well-known mindfulness exercise of savouring eating a raisin. Don't be in a rush.

As we begin to be more in charge of our choices around taste, we might change our dietary habits and feel we can be more in tune with finding out what really works for us, what food makes us bloated or does not suit our skin, notice too much salt or sugar in food. We might go on to make environmental choices, perhaps to eat less meat or more sustainable food. We might feel we can be more in charge of not over or under eating when we feel calm and easy.

Panoramic vision

Much of our brain is organised around vision. Rather like the fact we don't hear just with our ears but with our eardrums and our brains, we don't just see with the front of our eyes; our eyes receive light that travels to the back of them, where it is turned into the signals that go through our brains to the visual cortex where we interpret what we see. This acceptance of receiving vision rather than doing it can take a lot of strain out of our visual pathways. Take a moment to expand what you see and not just focus on the book or the screen, the letter or word but try to also see the big picture. Staying visually awake can help us notice when our minds wander.

Seeing the bigger picture is worth considering not just philosophically but visually. It turns out that only 5 per cent of our vision is designed for crystal clear focus – 95 per cent is for peripheral, or what we call panoramic, vision. This panoramic vision is seeing the height, the width and the depth, the colour and the shape of the space around us. Being in panoramic activates our parasympathetic system rather than being over-focused and stuck in the sympathetic system. Depth is something worth considering, as we usually see in panoramic depth when we feel relaxed and confident, safe and sound. Rather like that top of the mountain feeling or being by the sea, the sense

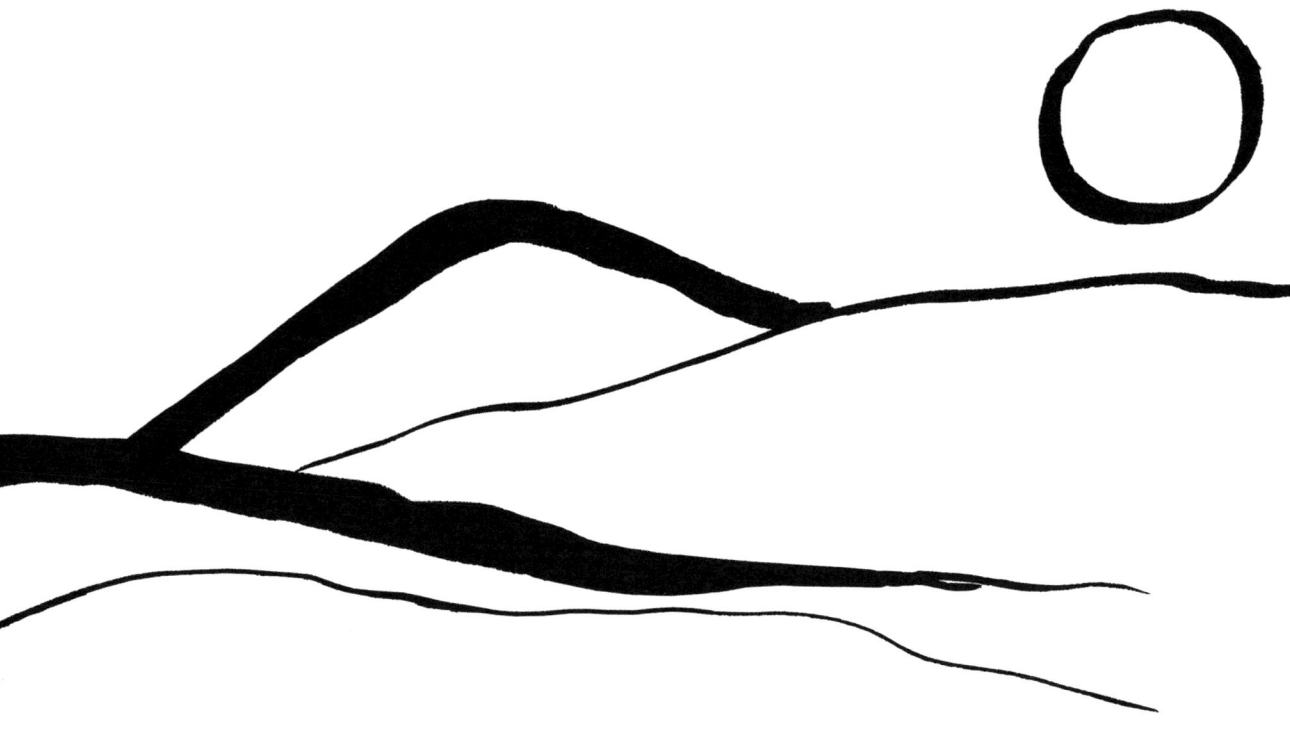

of seeing the bigger picture can keep our lives in perspective. It helps us see the wood and the trees. Remember, our eyes contain humours, so it's good to have a twinkle in them now and then.

If you are short-sighted, notice the space behind what you have chosen to focus on. If you are long-sighted, notice the space between you and whatever you have chosen to focus on. Noting spatial awareness is an aspect of vision that can make a big difference to our sense of ease. There are lots of very interesting books on vision, from Aldous Huxley's *The Art of Seeing*, to Peter Grunwald's *Eyebody*.

20-20-20 Variety and vision

There is a useful computer rule for eyes called 20-20-20. Every 20 minutes take 20 seconds to stop and look 20 metres away (or as far as possible) into a wider field, resting your eyes from over-focusing. It can be good to think, every 20 minutes I will stand up and stretch or walk around, every hour I will have a slightly longer break and lie down perhaps for 10 minutes to recover a sense of ease, avoiding letting pain get set in.

Palming

Lots of advice is given these days about not staring at the screen for too long. It can be very positive to just rest your eyes by closing them regularly. A great little holiday for our eyes is palming.

1. Find somewhere comfortable to sit – maybe where you can easily rest your elbows on something, like a table.

2. Let your head gently rest in your hands, covering the whole eye socket with your palms so there is absolutely no light at all.

3. Give yourself time to see into the dark, you can close your eyes, letting yourself really absorb the restfulness of the dark and ease.

4. Stay for a while and when you are ready, gently take your head away from your hands and gradually blink your eyes back to the present and the light.

5. Notice how your vision is now, can you see more clearly? Is the room brighter? Are your thoughts calmer?

Eye-strain tips

1. Avoid squeezing your eyes when you think.

2. Avoid frowning and staring all the time.

3. Let yourself remember what your eyes feel like when you laugh and smile.

4. Keep blinking when you are working at the computer or looking at your phone.

5. Buy some pinhole glasses to give your eyes a rest from regular glasses, they can also help you develop your panoramic vision.

6. Remember to have good light when you are reading or writing.

Vision: tracking

Our eyes have muscles that move them in their sockets. It's easy to get stuck and not move our eyes freely. Lots of traditions like yoga and tai chi include eye tracking and movement and have made the all-important connection between our vision and how our head moves. Try moving your eyes to the side and notice that your head can follow naturally. If you fix your focus in one place while your head can still move, you can notice that the quality of the movement is more restricted.

1. Follow your index finger with your eyes as you make a clock circle in front of you, going both clockwise and anticlockwise.

2. Try sending your eyes from side to side from 3 o'clock to 9 o'clock and back again several times. Do this following with your head and then again while keeping your head still and just moving your eyes.

3. Track your eyes diagonally. Doing this consciously can be a great way to help release your neck muscles and your eyes will feel more awake.

It is surprising how much we can get stuck looking a certain way, especially if one eye is stronger than the other. These sorts of exercises are also included in books that work on strengthening your eyesight. Some therapies, such as EMDR – Eye Movement Desensitisation and Reprocessing – use eye movements to unlock emotional tension.

Finding Quiet Strength

Walking and seeing
Really registering what we see means we can start to notice how much we can enjoy colour, shape and pattern contrasts and how much that can make a difference.

It can be interesting to choose moments to vary the tempo of your walk, take new routes and notice if you can keep the balance of being with yourself and with the environment.

Having a few visual reminders or pictures on your desk can be fun – postcards of landscapes, Chinese warriors, whatever works for you.

Regularly registering seeing and the world moving when you are walking, rather than looking at the ground, is very useful. This can help us unlock stuck thoughts, let them go and move on. Receive and see the big picture.

Hearing

We all probably know the feeling of hearing the beginning of a song that changes our mood and revitalises our sense of energy and optimism. Hearing is another sense that can be so helpful in terms of regulation. Lots of people describe how quiet birdsong and music have helped them to find ease under the pressure of difficult times. It is easy to focus on a sound that irritates us, but thinking of sound in depth and considering the ambient sound of the room we are in helps us to feel more spacious and easy.

Soft sounds

1. Try rubbing your thumb and fingers near your ears and register the close-up sound.

2. Move your hands out to the side and around you, still making the sound to give yourself a sense of panoramic hearing and space.

Tuning into quiet

Tuning into quiet can sometimes turn out to be quite noisy. We might hear our own mental chatter, become focused on an irritating noise from our computers or neighbours. This is when being able to choose what we pay attention to or identifying where we have a choice to change things can be so important.

Sound and vision can be triggers of the nervous system to go into a startle pattern. Remember what it's like when a lorry bumps loudly next to us, or a car alarm goes off. Our nervous systems automatically sense danger, so being able to recognise this reaction and restore our sense of quiet and safety is hugely important, not just for ourselves but for everyone around us too.

When we understand these ancient survival responses, we are so much more able to navigate them. Have a repertoire of lovely things to listen to that make you happy – birdsong, rivers, songs and music of all kinds are such an important part of returning to ease. You might find just having your own playlist of songs, or stories that you enjoy, or register and savour your favourite radio programme rather than just having your own mental radio as background noise all the time. Enjoy how natural noises change throughout the day and night, we need different sounds at different times.

Touch as reassurance

Touch often gets rather left out of the picture as we rush around grabbing items with our hands, so how pleasant it is to take time to enjoy touch. It is good to remember our whole body responds to touch; we often use it when we reassure others and we can include this friendly contact to ourselves and the way it can connect us to the moment. Touch can tune us into movement and the way we breathe.

The anchor of touch can be very helpful. It's wonderful to connect with hands-on work in an Alexander lesson context, as touch can be re-educational as well as reassuring, introducing us to ways through which we have held ourselves and by which we can release through a teacher's touch. There are many other helpful modalities of learning through touch and movement, such as Feldenkrais and Eutony, to tune you into being light and easy with your whole self in terms of structure and movement.

Backs of the hand

Slide the backs of your hands onto the sides of your neck. See if you can sense your neck being free with a little hint of the expansion and release of breathing. Noticing that breathing through your nose is good and can allow these waves of movement to and from the belly, through the whole body in response to the diaphragm moving freely as you breathe.

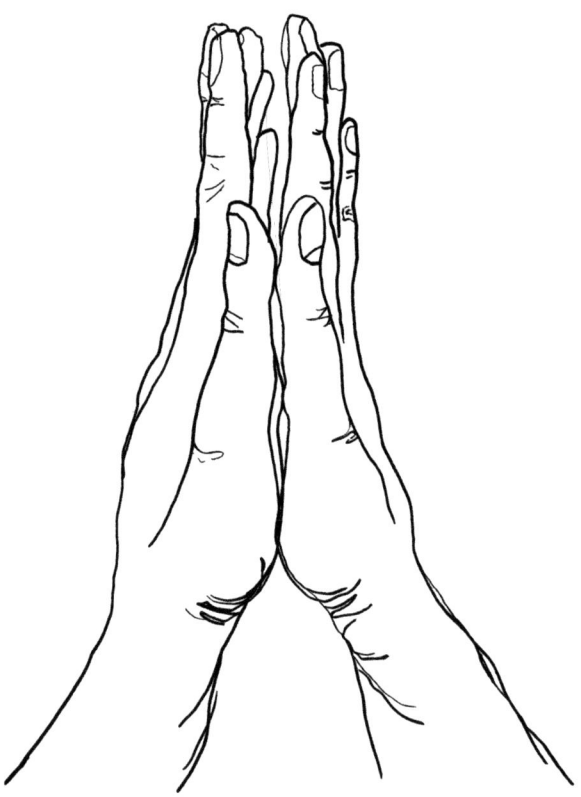

Touch can be a strong anchor to grounding

1. In sitting, try putting your hands on the top crests of your pelvis and very gently press down and let this connect you to your sitting bones, to find if the weight is even. You can do this in standing to get a very direct connection to your feet.

2. In sitting gently, press your hands on your knees and sense the release into your feet.

3. Gently place a hand on the top of your head, let the weight be light and feel the connection to your sitting bones releasing down and your head gently connecting up to your hand.

Finding Quiet Strength

Sensing breath and movement through touch

1. Try putting one hand on your lower belly – this is the part of your abdominal wall that is below your navel. See if this area expands and releases as you breathe. Let your hand stay there for a few breaths so you can really absorb the sense of the movement and the return to safety it introduces. We often hold tension in this lower abdomen area. This area stores long-term worries and concerns by fixing and tensing. Releasing brings us back to the rest and digest state in the nervous system.

2. Try putting your other hand on your solar plexus, this is the area just above the navel, and see if this expands and releases as you breathe. Again, stay for a few moments to absorb the ease this gives you.

3. Next, put your other hand on your sternum, over your heart and lungs, and allow this upper torso area to tune you into the rib cage expanding and relaxing as you breathe.

4. Next, slide your hands under your armpits. See if you can sense movement of expansion and release sideways. See if you can notice your shoulders and upper arms responding to this inner movement of the diaphragm and the lungs. This upper torso area doesn't need to take great gulping breaths but gently be available to the feeling of breathing as movement. Notice when this quiet movement is available to you and when it is not. For example, when someone is irritating you, it can make all the difference to your patience to allow movement back in your torso.

The comfort of touching your face

1. It can be very comforting to put your hands on your face around your jaw. Allow your jaw to release into your hands so your back teeth are apart.

2. Gently touch your lips and let your tongue be light and easy. Again, all these gestures help our nervous system to regulate and return to calm and a feeling of reassurance and safety.

Temperature and energy

Temperature makes a huge difference to us. Wim Hof's cold-water work is inspiring. He uses cold showers and cold-water swimming to help people work on breathing deeply and freely even under external pressures.
The results include people finding more resilience in facing life's pressures. Sometimes just splashing our face with cold water can be a tonic (better than too much coffee) if we are flagging and need to keep going. Cold showers and cold-water swims are very popular these days for regulating mental health as well as working on energy. Sometimes snuggling up to be warm on the sofa or in bed can help us feel safe and protected.
It's important to not overheat, or be too cold for too long.

Pressure points

These are areas that can almost go numb then feel very sore when we press them, so go gently and you can wake yourself up in these areas in a kind and informative way.

1. Gently rub the base of your skull at the back, and around behind your ears. The muscles here are most important and connect into great the depth of core muscles close to the spine that facilitate and support the big muscles of movement across the body.

2. Press gently and rub your temples.

3. Press gently on either side of the top of your nose.

4. Press gently on your jaw joints just in front of your earholes to help release tension there.

5. Press gently into the base of your thumb near your wrist. This is often thought to be useful for headaches and gut pain.

6. Press gently on either side of the base of your neck and then on the tops of your shoulders, give yourself a little massage. (Even better, have a massage now and then as they can be so enjoyable, helpful and therapeutic.)

Finding Quiet Strength

Connecting to touch

1. Rubbing your hands together can be enlivening, then stroking them up and down your arms, legs and torso, across your shoulders and your face and head, then end by giving yourself a hug – and someone else a hug when that is possible too. It's great to sense your hands are being touched as well as what they are touching.

2. Lightly tapping your hands and face and body in a gentle way can also be good for the restoration of energy and tranquillity.

Seeing, breathing & balancing. Connecting to our Dark Earth + Bright Sky.

Integration

Creating a new relationship with our embodiment means we can be much more consciously in charge of our lives in a deeper way. Enjoying a sense of restoring ourselves to ease includes receiving and enjoying information from our senses. Tuning in on a regular basis can give us the sense of befriending and listening to ourselves and the world around us in a more balanced way.

A metaphor to consider is the driver as the mind, the carriage as the body and the horses as the emotions. When they are all in harmony the journey goes easily, but every now and then we need to pay attention to one aspect or another to bring ourselves back to harmony. Which part of the nervous system's messages are organising our behaviour when our emotions, thoughts and muscles get fixed in agitation or fear? Integrating our awareness of the senses, movement and breath means we are more in charge of the horses.

Absorb the good. Recognise when you can feel calm, comfortable and easy, letting yourself really absorb this, so you can return to this feeling whenever you need to. Remember that seeing, breathing and balancing restores ease.

Connecting: the balance of life's energy
We are what we repeatedly do. Aristotle

When we can self-regulate, it is easier to see the big picture of our lives. Balance is important structurally as well as for our overall health in terms of how we balance our lives energetically in the long term, too. The burdens we carry in our minds or our shoulders can be hard to let go of, everyday worries become difficult to process if we don't regularly return to ease. Our energy is restored by resting as well as being easy, poised and having a sense of equilibrium throughout the day. This requires us not to see rest in terms of being lazy but as a long-term resolve, a vital part of balancing our physical and mental lives, avoiding burnout and anxiety.

Work
If your work requires sitting down for long periods of time, see if you can make your setup beneficial to you. Make sure your feet are on the ground, your sitting bones are on the chair, your knees are lower than your hips. Make sure, when you are working with purpose, it is not at the expense of breathing freely and easily. Take regular breaks to stretch, walk around, have a glass of water, look out into the distance – in other words, break regularly enough so that habits of heaviness, fixing or tension don't build up without recognising them.

Rest
Rest can be taking a moment to breathe, to see the room around you and return to balance in your body. Rest can just mean changing: a change is as good as… Open the door, notice the weather, go for a walk or take some time to lie down in semi-supine. Many of us who love our work can also forget how important it is to rest, think about something else and have a holiday to keep a sense of proportion and perspective. It is easy to think everything is super important if we forget to notice the stars.

Play
This is a word that has a great sense of music and movement. Remembering to have **fun** is important when we are talking about regulating our nervous systems. Through play we allow ourselves a sense of spontaneity, an approach that it is important not to lose. Play can be thought of as a quality of moving; when we have play in our muscles there is a sense of flow and ease in the structure.

Curiosity

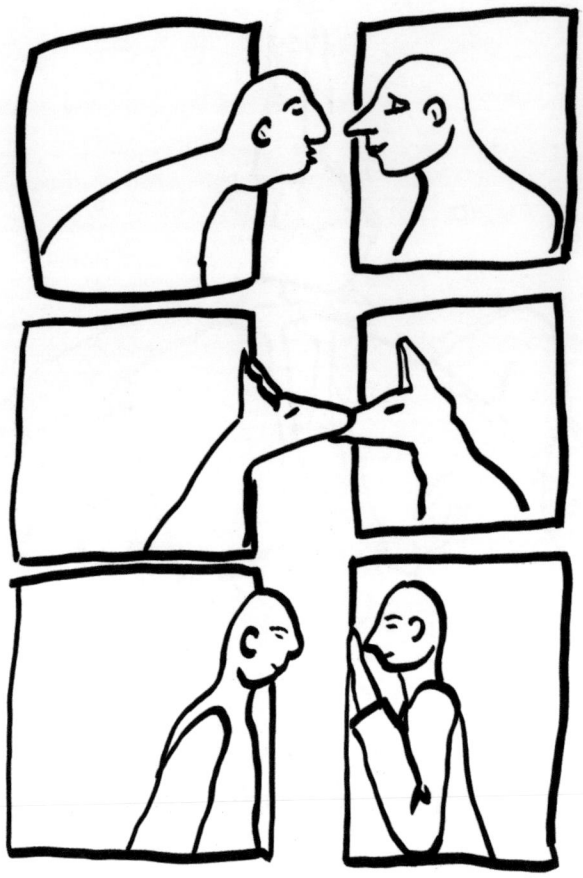

Co-regulation

Self-regulation is when we are able to organise ourselves back to a chosen easy state. Co-regulation is when we can negotiate and talk things through with others peacefully, even under pressure, and allow ourselves to be respected and respectful, helped and comforted by others and help and comfort them in turn. We might notice these two aspects of ourselves are totally intertwined. When we interact easily and skilfully with others, we feel enriched and so do they. Co-regulation implies learning to let go of fighting and defence.

Allowing our nervous systems to return to balance, through a sense of support from our fellow humans, is when we can experience this sense of cooperation. In the discipline of nonviolent communication, NVC practitioners demonstrate two aspects of ourselves with two hand puppets, one is a jackal and one is a giraffe. It's a clever way to notice where we are

Curiosity

coming from in communication. Sometimes taking a moment to find our capacity to choose is useful. To find empathy and compassion towards each other usually requires us to think: are we part of the solution or part of the problem? Notice the embodiment of these interactions – losing our ground, neck tightening, breath shortening, losing our panoramic vision when we feel under pressure with someone else.

Knowing your own **boundaries** is also important. Boundary oaks used to express the division between different peoples' fields. If you see them in the country, they are so much better than walls or fences, as they each have space around them, creating an open sense of strength. We all sense a great strength in ourselves when instead of feeling in competition with others we feel inspired and supported by them. We embody our choice to be kind to ourselves and others when we look after our boundaries.

Finding Quiet Strength

Move together
In Alexander work there is the partnership of the hands-on work and the form this can take is gentle guidance in movement from the teacher. This is usually focused on everyday movements, alongside the beautiful release work of semi-supine.

Sticking and yielding

In tai chi there is a thought-provoking principle called yielding. This is explored working with a partner. It's a great metaphor for a cooperative relationship. You can practise this with a partner with your hand on their wrists, sticking to them as they move. This sticking is useful for listening to touch and movement. If you or your partner starts to push or use too much weight, the principle of yielding comes into play, where you yield and release rather than responding with pushing. It's rather like stepping back and deciding not to engage in another person's aggression, which is invaluable for cooperative interaction.

In pairs, finding a respectful mutual resistance in each other's contact can be effective for finding your ground, finding your back and finding a flow and ease in moving together. Notice whether you are the submissive one or indeed the pushy one! Finding a cooperative ease is the aim. Many forms of moving together in tai chi, yoga, dance, running, walking can be great for being together in a friendly, nonverbal way. It's also true that some conversations are best had when walking together outside, as talking can be easier with motion in the open air.

Education: learning new skills, seeing new things, widening our comfort zones

American philosopher and educationalist John Dewey said, 'When a reasonably adequate part of a new generation has become properly coordinated we shall have assurance for the first time that men and women in the future will be able to stand on their own two feet, equipped with satisfactory psychophysical equilibrium to meet with readiness, confidence and happiness, instead of with fear and discontent, the buffeting and contingencies of their surroundings.'

Taking the work of wellbeing into education is as essential as people learning how to add up, read and write. Giving young people the tools to look after their mental and physical health, to understand how to make useful choices, find their potential and how to achieve it, seems fundamental. To let young people grow upwards and not get downhearted.

When education is cooperative rather than a competition, it can convey a big message of creatively looking after yourself, each other and the world. Dewey also spoke about how consciously connecting to self-regulation through Alexander work had helped him be able to hold an opinion, then to change his mind when the evidence changed. Letting go of outdated modes of operating or opinions or even old hurts can be very liberating.

Of course, lots of schools and colleges are doing wonderful work, but for more information on wellbeing in education see *The Ready List in Education* (www.thereadylist.com).

Curiosity

Education and chairs
It's important to have a think about what you sit on.

We are often sitting on chairs that make it almost impossible to maintain balance, coordination or ease. The Alexander world has an ongoing campaign for the design of school chairs to be more considered. Often we expect children to sit on chairs for hours a day that wouldn't be passed by teachers' unions. When will we wake up to see that this is not unlike the thinking that cigarettes weren't dangerous? Children and adults need to sit on chairs that are the right height for them, chairs that do not make your knees higher than your hips. This is because it's impossible to maintain an easy balance on your sit bones if your knees are higher than your hip joints when sitting.

At home, if your chair is not great, try balancing the back legs of it on two large books to create a forward tilt. You can also buy wedge shaped cushions that help you to balance easily while sitting. Once this is more familiar it will be easier to sit well on horizontal chairs.

Chairs that tip back should be banned or binned.

Creativity and purpose

Empowering our energy

Creativity and purpose

Efficacy

Creativity can play a huge part in everything we do and can help us solve problems. It is so easy to put creativity low on the list of our priorities, and yet when we are creative and use our imagination, we often feel much better.

From cave paintings to making musical instruments, a core part of being human is having a creative mind and experiencing the fulfilment that comes with using it. Creativity is not about trying to get things right but finding a sense of experimentation and flow. If we can include noticing our embodied signals when we are creative this can unlock massive potential as well as give our life meaning.

Often, we only associate creativity with crafts or arts: drawing, writing, gardening. All of these are hugely important in balancing our lives, but it is also important to be creative about our daily lives, as this can help us avoid putting our backs out, getting anxious when we are involved in normal activities, as well as our creative outlets. Staying healthy, happy and easy can be an act of creativity that boosts our wellbeing with a sense of fulfilment and ease. This gives us a greater sense of efficacy and wellbeing when we come to our creative skills.

Seeing our daily experiences as a creative act makes us more effective humans in whatever we choose to do. A great step towards this can be choosing to be with ourselves in all activities. This purpose leads to poise – whether we are brushing our teeth, sitting at the computer or painting the Sistine Chapel.

Self-acceptance leads to self-development

Purpose, fulfilment and recognition are vital components of mental health. We see some successful people struggle with self-esteem. Working on acknowledging what we have achieved and enjoying the process of achieving means we can grow our skills healthily.

Sense of connection to creativity

A wonderful book on rediscovering your artistry applied to writing is *The Artist's Way* by Julia Cameron, which could apply to any creative discipline.

Creativity and purpose

The big messages for rediscovering creativity are 'morning pages' (a time you give yourself to practise creativity every day) and the 'artist's date' (making regular times to go out and be inspired by other people's work or nature). Having a practice buddy, a co-creator and motivator can help, because co-regulation inspires you to keep going and find the next step or idea.

Talent code

One major problem in learning can be the need to always get things right. This of course needs to be balanced by encouragement and humour. In his powerful book on growing skills, *The Talent Code*, Daniel Coyle looks at how often talent grows in areas where the conditions are right, rather like putting a tree into the right climate and soil conditions. These conditions turn out often to be in the way someone is coached to have a growth mindset rather than a self-punitive relationship with learning. It turns out that talented people tend not to punish themselves about getting things wrong but get interested in what they could change to make things easier. Great coaches engender this healthy mindset by encouraging their students' curiosity. Curiosity can be accompanied by drive and purpose.

This understanding helps us to develop a healthy relationship with the skill we are developing, unpack the different elements of it, be able to chunk it up into component parts and then bring the elements back to a sense of wholeness. Understanding that this attitude to learning is integrated with how we embody our thoughts is crucial. It means we can notice when it's time to stop and take a break if we are getting despondent, overwhelmed or uninspired.

It is good to know that most skilful people have bad days and that momentary blocks are natural. Notice how skilled performers or sportspeople approach their discipline. Dame Judi Dench, Pavarotti, David Bowie, Lewis Hamilton and most of our heroes embody the grace of a constructive mindset that's integrated with the building of their skill. Our coordination improves if we feel optimistic, creative, curious and purposeful.

Sustainable work

1. Take time to think about what you are working on and what mindset and body sense you would like to focus on.

2. Don't work for too long, stay fresh and take little regular breaks to stretch, rest and reboot your imagination.

3. Work on being inspired by others rather than being intimidated, know your worth and sense your ground.

4. Enjoy bringing your wholehearted attention to what you are doing.

5. Remember the three questions: Am I seeing? Am I breathing? Am I balancing? (See page 36)

Creativity and purpose

Stage fright

Stage fright is often characterised by a tightness of breath, feeling sweaty and slightly out of control.

1. Experiment with running up and down stairs then running through your performance so you can work on how to notice that you can deal with feeling out of breath without associating it with fear or anxiety.

2. Regulate by lengthening your out breaths and letting your in breaths be received easily and fully with a springy light rib cage. Breathe in confidence, breathe out fear.

Creative connection: nature's tempo

Perhaps the most important connection we can all make is with the environment. Deepening our relationship with nature can be healing, not only connecting to the world around us but letting it connect to us by tuning in. Being inspired to embody the qualities of nature, how a river flows, how a tree embodies its structure, how the mountain stands. Many ancient traditions are inspired by this deep link. This allows us to have a sense of having roots, a free trunk, broad shoulders and a structure that grows downwards and upwards and outwards.

Consciously notice what is there; maybe focus on one flower, on a leaf, then look out on a big picture and landscape. This precious resource is available to most of us through local walks, parks, canals; urban street walks can reap great wonders too. Absorbing the weather, the sounds, the movement of trees, rivers, the sea or the activity of wildlife, inspires us to help in whatever way we can to conserve it.

Conservation is positive, gentle action. There are lots of ways this can be done without burning ourselves out or losing heart. This brings a natural tempo into our lives, for example feeding the birds, making this one of your hopeful morning rituals, being sure you really enjoy it and the movement and ease of not rushing it.

Creativity and purpose

The garden classroom

There are many movements in education to help children connect to the environment. Inspiring children to look after a window box, feed the birds, join a gardening group, apply for an allotment. As well as this, help them to choose not to use too much plastic. When we are easy, embodied and open-minded, we start to make good choices not just for ourselves, but to inspire each other to take action and find wonder.

Courage and conclusion

A quiet revolution

Courage and conclusion

A new relationship with our embodiment

It's very understandable that a lot of tension and disconnection gets normalised in our fast and changing modern world. We stop recognising that we are walking around with all this pressure and forget that we have the skill through choice to release it. In the animal kingdom we see releases of tension that are spontaneous and relatively quick. We humans tend to hold on to patterns of fear and defence, with difficult consequences.

We all hope to live life to the full, seize the day, expand our comfort zones, accept change, take action, relate well to ourselves and others, learn and adapt. Sometimes we just can't – even getting up can feel like an act of bravery. When this happens, it's time to stop, rest and think. Are we trying too hard? Are we too tired? Have we lost our vital spark? Do we need to work things out, or just go for a walk? Is our life too complicated? We all need short-term and long-term strategies. Most of us will find it helpful to rediscover the often lost and unidentified skills of embodied courage, optimism and calm. We can recognise how we think and how we can over-think, how we lose touch with our senses and the impact of this on our emotional health.

There are so many modalities available, wonderful practices to connect to ourselves in a positive way. Here I have written about some of the influences that I teach and have become my practice. It is important to keep an open mind and see that different things work for us at different times. Different disciplines open us to new ideas and allow us to find our repertoire.

Finding Peace is our Strength

Life is not about getting someone else's model right but finding what works for us at this time, growing and deepening our life skills when we can. There will be times when we need to find someone to help us develop our skills. They might be a teacher, a therapist or simply an inspirational person. All of the practices I have spoken about in this book you can do at home or with a teacher or at a regular class.

It is important to have resources to rest, renew and restore ourselves. When we can begin to repattern our reactions we begin a new creative relationship with our lives; one of connection not correction, to befriend and be kind to ourselves. Let's learn to live life in the moment with peace and purpose.

Finding Quiet Strength

Finding peace is our strength
Inspirations

A core element of this work is based on FM Alexander's working principles which create an operational framework for thinking in activity about the integration of the mind, body and emotions. Finding quiet strength combines this understanding with the strength and ease found in yoga and with the philosophy, freedom and release found in chi kung and tai chi.

These ancient traditions help us recognise the signals of threat that trigger old patterns of defence and fear, helping us to restore a sense of being grounded and centred. Current research in neuroscience backs up these practices and shows that we humans are able to consciously re-pattern our nervous systems by organising our thinking, regulating our breath and movement in response to the stimuli of life. New approaches in the therapeutic world are recognising and identifying how 'the body keeps the score.' Through this understanding we can indirectly affect our emotions through releasing the signals of fear and trauma and embody the elements of safety.

This means we can learn to regulate ourselves by knowing how to cue-in safety. We get better at being present with what we are doing, easier under pressure, and we start not minding so much about getting things 'wrong'. These are powerful and relevant skills for modern life, for learning, and for moments of challenge. I have hoped to draw together some of these different skills that can help us find a sense of wholeness, so we can weather the storms, let go of old hurts and recover a feeling of being 'at home' with ourselves. This can help us expand our comfort zones, look after ourselves and each other in our beautiful world and learn how to look after it.

Judith Kleinman AGSM MSTAT

Judith originally trained as a musician at the Guildhall School of Music and Drama, going on to be a member of English National Opera and performed with LSO, London Classical Players and at the National Theatre.

The mind-body connection involved in practising and performing music fascinated her. In order to explore this connection more deeply, Judith trained to be an Alexander Technique teacher with Patrick Macdonald and Shoshanna Kaminitz, qualifying in 1989, then went on to train to be a tai chi and yoga teacher in London.

She is part of the Alexander team at the Royal College of Music and head of department at the Junior Royal Academy of Music. She is also co-head of training at LCATT, The London Centre for Alexander Technique and Training. Recently she has been a visiting teacher at the London School of Musical Theatre.

For the last twenty years Judith has collaborated with Sue Merry to build connections between the worlds of Alexander and education and created a thoughtful training for AT teachers interested in working in that world.

Judith has also written several books including *The Alexander Technique for Musicians* with Peter Buckoke (published by Bloomsbury, 2013), and more recently *The Alexander Technique for Young Musicians* with Fuensanta Zambrana and Peter Buckoke (2019), a reference book aimed at Key Stage 3 students. Further publications include *Alexander in Secondary and Tertiary Education (2018)*, a book for teachers looking to integrate Alexander principles in their teaching.

Judith developed *Finding Quiet Strength* to unite the influences of the various disciplines she works with. She regularly writes articles, gives workshops and talks in the UK, Europe and the USA, both to the wider public and the music and education worlds.

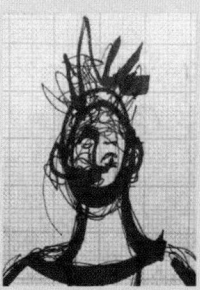

Further reading

Books on wellbeing and creativity
Just One Thing, Rick Hansen (New Harbinger Publications, 2011)
The Artist's Way, Julia Cameron (Souvenir Publications, 1992)
Emotional Intelligence, Daniel Goleman (Bloomsbury, 1996)
The Talent Code, Daniel Coyle (Arrow, 2010)
Inner Game of Tennis, Timothy Gallwey (Pan Books, 1975)
Waking the Tiger: Healing Trauma, Peter Levine with Anna Frederick (North Atlantic Books, 1997)

Alexander books
Alexander Technique for Actors, Penny O'Connor (Nick Hern Books, 2021)
The Alexander Technique for Musicians, Judith Kleinman, Peter Buckoke (Bloomsbury, 2013)
Dance and the Alexander Technique, Rebecca Nettl-Fiol, Luc Vanier (Illinois, 2011)
The Alexander Technique for Young Musicians, Judith Kleinman, Fuensanta Zambrana and Peter Buckoke (published independently, 2019)
Alexander in Secondary and Tertiary Education, Judith Kleinman (published independently *2018*)

Neuroscience
The Brain that Changes Itself, Norman Doidge (Penguin, 2008)
The Polyvagal Theory, Steven Porges (W.W. Norton, 2011)
Anchored: How to Befriend Your Nervous System Using Polyvagal Theory, Deb Dana (Sounds True, 2020)
The Body Keeps the Score, Bessel van der Kolk (Penguin, 2014)

The body
Gut, Giulia Enders (Scribe UK, 2017)
Your Body, Your Voice, Theodore Dimon (North Atlantic Books, 2011)
Anatomy in Motion, Theodore Dimon (North Atlantic Books, 2021)
Breath, James Nestor (Penguin, 2020)

Useful websites

www.findingquietstrength.com
www.alexandernow.org
www.thereadylist.com
www.artofbreathing.eu

To find a local Alexander teacher
www.alexandertechnique.co.uk

Find a local tai chi class
www.taichiunion.com

Online tai chi classes
www.livingmovement.com

Find a local yoga class
www.bwy.org.uk

Apps
think up – flow balance and ease
@findingquietstrength